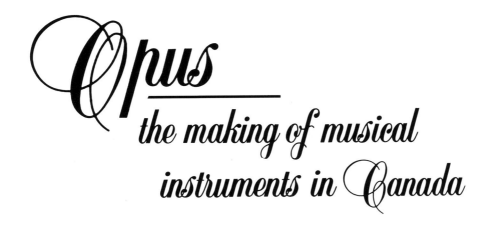

Opus
the making of musical instruments in Canada

Carmelle Bégin

with the assistance of
Constance Nebel

Canadian Museum of Civilization

Canadian Cataloguing in Publication Data

Canadian Museum of Civilization

Opus: the making of musical instruments in Canada

Issued also in French under title: Opus, la facture instrumentale au Canada.
Includes bibliographical references.
ISBN 0-660-14006-3

1. Musical instruments — Exhibitions. 2. Musical instruments — Construction — Canada — Exhibitions. 3. Canadian Museum of Civilization — Musical instrument collections — Exhibitions.
I. Bégin, Carmelle. II. Title. III. Title: The making of musical instruments in Canada.

ML462.H8C3213 1992   784.19'074'714221   C92-099758-9

 PRINTED IN CANADA

Published by the
Canadian Museum of Civilization
Hull, Quebec
J8X 4H2

Project Coordinator: Madeleine Choquette
Assistant Researcher: Constance Nebel
Translator: Terrance Hughes
English Editor: Catherine Cunningham-Huston
Head of Design and Production: Deborah Brownrigg
Desktop Publishing: Francine Boucher

Terminological Research: Lise Bellefeuille
Bibliographic Research: Kevin James

Photography:
Rolf Bettner photographed most of the instruments. The following individuals took the photos on the pages indicated:
Jean-Pierre Camus, pp. 24, 30, 39, 45, 75, 76 and 93
Harry Foster, pp. 8, 66 (on right), 67 and 91 (on right) and flap
Carmelle Bégin, pp. 51 (on left), 56 and 126
Barbara Zuchowicz, pp. 12 and 26 (on right)
Jean-Pierre Beaudin, p. 68
Yves Beaupré, p. 94
Steve Darby, p. 11
Gold Photography (Calgary, Alberta), p. 5
Merle Toole, p.107

Cover:
Steel-string guitar by Michael Dunn (photo by Rolf Bettner)

Back cover:
Celtic harp by Tim Hobrough; drum set by Ayotte Drum Company and cymbals by Sabian Ltd; harpsichord by Yves Beaupré

Canadä

Contents

Foreword

I have always enjoyed my visits to the world's great collections of musical instruments, such as the one at the Metropolitan Museum in New York and the one in Bruges, Belgium. And I have often wondered whether anything similar could be mounted in Canada. After all, music and the making of musical instruments have held a place of some importance in the development of all civilized peoples, whether in ancient Egypt, seventeenth-century Cremona or modern-day central Africa.

While museums have been preserving rare instruments from the past, very few have been concerned with collecting recently made instruments that best reflect the musical aspirations of our society as we near the end of this century.

The Canadian-made instruments presented in this collection demonstrate a commitment to excellence. I am delighted to see that these instruments of outstanding craftsmanship are being brought before the public, and I hope this book will stimulate further interest in an area that deserves our support and our encouragement.

I wish great success to this truly worthwhile endeavour.

Mario Bernardi
Music Director
Calgary Philharmonic Orchestra

Preface

The Latin word *opus* means "work." Used by composers to number their musical works (for example, Beethoven's Sonata for Piano, Opus 106), the term is also popular with makers of musical instruments. It not only provides a useful identification system, but also makes it possible to locate a work within a corpus.

"Luthier" refers to a maker of stringed instruments, particularly in the violin family. The term "instrument maker," on the other hand, will designate all other artisans of musical instruments.

This book features over one hundred musical instruments produced in Canada by contemporary luthiers and instrument makers. Now part of the permanent collection of the Canadian Museum of Civilization, the instruments were acquired over the past seventeen years, and some were specially commissioned for the Museum's exhibition *Opus*, which this publication is designed to complement.

This book is by no means an exhaustive survey of instrument making in Canada. It depicts an art which, despite a century of very slow development, has experienced a revival in the last two decades. The selection of instruments illustrates this new phenomenon.

As much information as possible is given to satisfy both the specialist and the amateur. Accordingly, there are descriptions of the instruments, biographical notes on the artisans, technical details, photographs taken during visits to workshops, and commentary relevant to the particular section in which each instrument is located.

Lastly, it should be noted that as the exhibition behind this publication highlights the Museum's treasure of crafts, the selection of objects does not include instruments that would be more suitable in a folk art exhibition.

Introduction

The foremost collections of musical instruments in the world are made up of historic and ethnographic instruments. The systematic collection of such vestiges of musical life began only in the nineteenth century, when François-Joseph Fétis established the core of the Musée instrumental de Bruxelles collection. At the turn of the century, two Englishmen, Arnold Dolmetsch and Francis W. Galpin, assembled large collections of instruments, along with historic documents and details concerning the making and use of the instruments. These and other collections in European and American museums gave impetus to research in organology, the study of musical instruments. They are valuable sources of documentation for luthiers and other instrument makers.

There are several hundred musical instruments of ethnographic interest in the collection of the Canadian Museum of Civilization. Over the past seventeen years, newer instruments have been added to the collection, which now ranges from reproductions of medieval instruments to modern ones. These additions to the Museum's collection were prompted by the widespread interest in early music that arose in Canada and North America in general in the late 1960s. At the same time, the need for period instruments burgeoned, with the result that interest in the making of stringed and other instruments has grown steadily since then.

The more than fifty instrument makers featured in this book approach their art in different ways. Some have adopted a scientific, methodical, orderly approach, while others are more empirical, relying to varying degrees on intuition. Some instrument makers have received professional training at major schools or from master luthiers.

Robert Campbell, playing guitar made by Linda Manzer, 1992.

Still others are self-taught and have acquired extensive knowledge by conducting research in museums, archives and libraries the world over.

Opus deals with two types of instruments: European instruments used in the performance of "art music," and ethnocultural instruments used in the performance of traditional music. The first type includes reproductions of instruments from the Middle Ages, the Renaissance, and the baroque and classical periods, as well as modern instruments. The other type encompasses instruments from within and outside the Americas.

The book focuses on four themes — the making, history, aesthetics and symbolism of musical instruments — each illustrated by particular instruments. Special emphasis has been placed on the various stages in the development of instrument makers, their sources of documentation and inspiration, and their concerns in light of the changing needs of modern society. In particular, the chapters devoted to aesthetics and symbolism provide fresh insights into the art of luthiers and other instrument makers by highlighting a number of little-known facets of this art. It is hoped that *Opus* will contribute to a fuller appreciation of the fine work of luthiers and instrument makers in Canada.

Instruments can be classified in one of four categories, depending on how the sound is produced. Victor Mahillon, a musicologist at the Musée instrumental de Bruxelles, devised this system, which was refined at the turn of the century by musicologists Erich von Hornbostel and Curt Sachs. It includes:

- idiophones, such as cymbals and bells, in which the vibration of the instrument itself produces the sound;
- aerophones, such as flutes and trumpets, in which sound is produced by air, usually in a tube;

- chordophones, such as violins and harps, whose strings vibrate when plucked, struck, rubbed or strummed; and
- membranophones, such as drums, in which a membrane vibrates.

   Unless otherwise indicated, the dimensions of the instruments are given as follows:
- **chordophones**: overall length, length by width of body, and height of sides or ribs;
- **aerophones** and **bows**: overall length, with the exception of the trumpet, for which the diameter of the bell is indicated; and
- **idiophones** and **membranophones**: diameter of the vibrating surface and height of the soundbox, depending on the instrument.

When Canada was still a colony, the task of repairing instruments or producing violins for music lovers fell to wood craftsmen such as cabinetmakers and carpenters. Today, instrument making is recognized as a profession in its own right and is taught in specialized schools and by masters in the field. Some artisans, like those interviewed for this book, begin as musicians and eventually learn the secrets of their craft. Thus, a violinist becomes a luthier; a harpsichordist begins making harpsichords; or a flautist turns to crafting flutes.

All these artisans, at some point in their training or career, need to consult various sources of documentation to learn how to make a particular type of instrument. For example, a luthier who specializes in medieval reproductions must rely on

Previous page: *Peter Mach examines the scroll on one of his instruments, 1992. The scroll on stringed instruments is reminiscent of the spiral shape of some seashells.*

Above: *Using a gouge to carve a viol head.*

illustrations for information on the construction, use and history of an instrument, as very few instruments from before the sixteenth century have survived. The artisan must also bear in mind that any reproduction, whether a painting, sculpture, illumination or engraving, will not reveal all of an instrument's features, such as the type of material used, the thickness of the various parts, or the tension of the strings.

More information is available on Renaissance instruments. Some details of manufacture are provided through instruments that have been preserved, and through various writings. For example, a mid-fifteenth-century manuscript by Henri Arnault de Zwolle, a physician and astrologer employed by the Duke of Burgundy, contains descriptions and drawings of some musical instruments of the period. Among a number of sixteenth-century books is the major three-volume treatise *Syntagma Musicum*, by German composer Michael Praetorius; the second volume, *De Organographia*, gives numerous details on the instruments of the time. Marin Mersenne's seventeenth-century

Harmonie universelle constitutes an encyclopaedia of music, with a major section on instruments.

Later periods offer plentiful evidence of musical life, and museum collections are rich in instruments of all types. However, the collections are not always representative of the instruments peculiar to these periods, as collectors have tended to preserve the most richly ornamented works. Finally, some instruments have been altered by repair or have been modernized.

Museums have enlisted the help of instrument makers to produce technical plans and drawings of instruments in their collections. These plans, which faithfully reproduce the various parts of the instruments, are a boon to researchers. Some luthiers prefer to draw their own plans from the original instrument and may even X-ray an instrument to reveal all its features.

Yet, despite a luthier's most meticulous efforts to reproduce a period instrument, the original materials are often no longer available and must be replaced by similar materials. With the ban on the importation of materials such as ivory and tortoise-shell, it is difficult, if not impossible, to reproduce certain instruments exactly. Some artisans use recycled materials, such as ivory from piano keys, or substitute synthetic products resembling the more precious substances.

Many Canadian instrument makers use indigenous woods. Maple, Sitka spruce and black cherry, for example, are ideal for the construction of many types of instruments, and the forests of British Columbia, eastern Ontario and southern Quebec are particularly rich sources of wood for stringed instruments. Some artisans find interesting materials in buildings that are being demolished, as wood from old house frames offers a number of attractive qualities, including dryness.

Other instruments or instrument parts are made exclusively of imported woods. Among the most popular are Brazilian rosewood and Pernambuco wood, and European spruce and boxwood. These woods offer numerous advantages, including flexibility, resistance to warping and to splitting when they are turned on a lathe, and superior acoustics. Unfortunately, the widespread fires in the Amazon forests are threatening the supply of rosewood; and the European woods that are popular because of their age, such as close-grained spruce, are becoming increasingly rare.

Instrument makers must respond to the changing musical tastes of their clientèle and the public. This principle has dictated the evolution of music and instrument making for centuries. Many luthiers agree that musical instruments are constantly changing and that there is always room for innovation and improvement—even on a Stradivarius violin, which is considered the ultimate in stringed instruments. Some artisans have unquestionably improved instruments by making them more mechanically stable and reducing the risks of warping and breaking, while at the same time preserving their intrinsic aesthetics and tone.

For these reasons, such instruments must be considered original, even if they imitate the style of an earlier period. Like Stradivari, who refused to copy the violins of Amati, his master, our Canadian instrument makers imbue their instruments with a totally original character. As can be seen throughout this book, this originality derives primarily from the inventiveness, sensitivity and professionalism of Canadian luthiers and instrument makers.

Medieval Instruments and Their Iconography

Opus 1 – Organistrum

The organistrum is the precursor of the hurdy-gurdy. In both instruments, sound is produced when the strings are rubbed by a crank-activated friction wheel. Because of the organistrum's large size, two musicians were required to play it: one to turn the crank and the other to actually play the instrument, using rotating keys. The keys thus came into contact with two strings, while a third string acted as a drone. The three strings were probably tuned to the tonic, the fifth and the octave, an arrangement well suited to the polyphony prevalent at the time, in which the voices moved in parallel fourths and fifths.

The instrument appears occasionally in twelfth-century sculptural reliefs in England, France and Spain. It was used in the cloisters to teach music, provide pitch for singers and accompany religious music.

Edward Turner based this organistrum on a twelfth-century bas-relief from the portico of San Miguel de Estella church in Santiago de Compostela, Spain. The reproduction displays a remarkable wealth of detail, including a carved griffin head, whose mouth opens onto the crank that activates the friction wheel.

Edward R. Turner

Edward Turner has enjoyed a rich and varied career. After studying architectural design and graphic arts at the École des Beaux-Arts de Montréal, he turned to making harpsichords and stringed instruments as a result of his interest in pre-nineteenth-century music and instruments. He devoted himself full-time to this endeavour after opening a workshop in Vancouver in 1971. He later went to work for the University of Edinburgh, where he conducted research and specialized in drawing instruments from the Russell collection of early keyboard instruments. Harpsichord makers around the world use his technical plans and drawings of the most important harpsichords in the collection.

Turner has played a significant role in the revival of instrument making in Canada. He has built several replicas of early instruments, including harpsichords, lutes and hurdy-gurdies. He has promoted instrument making through workshops and lectures in Canada and other countries around the world, including the People's Republic of China, which he visited in the early 1980s.

In 1985, Edward Turner resumed design and graphic arts. He created reproductions of historic aircraft for Expo 86 and has designed sailboats.

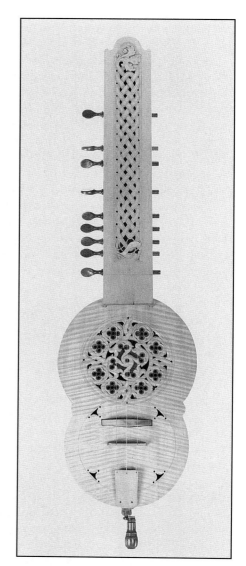

OPUS 1

Organistrum
By Edward R. Turner
Vancouver, British Columbia
1973
Ontario maple, European curly maple,
walnut, metal, gut
Overall length: 142 cm;
body: 56 x 36 cm; sides: 11 cm
CCFCS 74-246

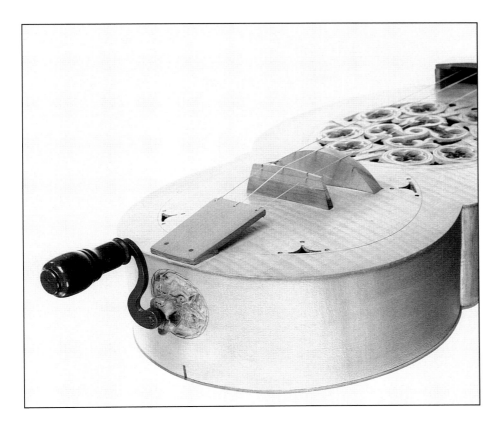

Ornamental detail at the base of the crank: the griffin, a mythical creature.

Opus 2 and 3 – Vitheles

The vithele was one of the most common bow instruments during the Middle Ages. It was played by nobles, peasants and jugglers alike, and was the favourite instrument of minstrels. Appearing at all festivities, it accompanied songs, dances and epic poems, alone or with a harp, psaltery, lute or recorder.

The vithele was held on the shoulder in much the same way as a violin, although a number of paintings show musicians seated with the instrument on their knees. The vithele's shape, number of strings and bow can vary greatly. While the instrument's origins are hard to pinpoint, the bow appears to have been used in Spain and Italy in the tenth century, based on the practice in Arab and Byzantine countries. In the eleventh century, the practice spread throughout Europe, and the medieval vithele appeared around this time. The instrument remained in use until the late fifteenth century, when it was gradually supplanted by instruments related to the viola da gamba and the violin.

Luthier Christopher Allworth refers to Opus 2 as a "medieval viol" to indicate that it has a lower tessitura and that it is held on the knees.

The instrument is based on an illumination in the twelfth-century York Psalter, which shows King David playing the harp surrounded by minstrels playing various stringed instruments (University of Glasgow, Ms. U.2.3). The entire instrument is painted with tempera. The back is bright red, and the ribs and peg box are covered with colourful Roman-style leaves. A wyvern, with a deer's head, bird's wings and serpent's tail, graces the tailpiece. Allworth reproduced these decorations from a thirteenth-century English manuscript in the British Museum.

Opus 3 is the smaller vithele. To build this tempera-painted replica, the luthier turned to an illumination in the thirteenth-century Bromholm Psalter and the books of the Trinity Apocalypse (Trinity College, Cambridge, Ms. R.16.2). The motifs on the tailpiece and the

OPUS 2

Vithele (medieval viol)
By Christopher Allworth
Halifax, Nova Scotia
1973
Swiss pine, maple, birch, willow, English yew, gut
Overall length: 83 cm; body: 53 x 27 cm; ribs: 8.2 cm
CCFCS 74-1276
Label: "Christopher Allworth, 1973, Auburn, Nova Scotia"

Below right: *The tailpiece depicts a wyvern.*

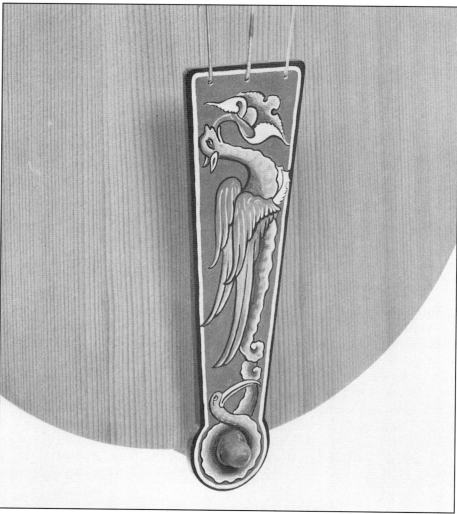

ribs are from two psalters preserved in the British Museum: The tailpiece bears a winged lion whose head is surmounted by a halo, a symbol of St. Mark the Evangelist as he appears in the Westminster Abbey Psalter (circa 1340); and the blue and gold motifs on the ribs of the instrument are inspired by the Luttrell Psalter.

OPUS 3

Vithele
By Christopher Allworth
Halifax, Nova Scotia
1974
Beech, pearwood, cherry, Swiss pine,
English yew, gold leaf, gut
Overall length: 73 cm; body: 42 x 19 cm;
ribs: 5 cm
CCFCS 74-1277
Label: "Christopher Allworth, 1974,
Auburn, Nova Scotia"

Opus 4 – Psaltery

The psaltery is a stringed instrument that enjoyed prominence during the Middle Ages. Its strings, stretched over a soundboard, are plucked with the fingers or a plectrum. In paintings, the psaltery is usually shown resting against the musician's chest or occasionally on the knees. The instrument was played throughout Europe from the eleventh to the early sixteenth century. Its development was influenced by the *quànun*, or Middle Eastern psaltery, which the Moors introduced into Spain around the twelfth century. The earliest instruments were square, rectangular or trapezoidal. Around the thirteenth century, there appeared a psaltery called the *instrumento di porco*, so named because of its curved shape resembling a pig's snout. The instrument shown here is a reproduction of this type of psaltery. The three small sides are decorated with a four-leaf motif painted with tempera and gold leaf.

OPUS 4

Psaltery
By Christopher Allworth
Halifax, Nova Scotia
1974
Birch, cedar, brass, gold leaf, feather quill
Overall length by width: 45 x 33 cm;
ribs: 6 cm
CCFCS 74-1278
Label: "Christopher Allworth maker
Yarmouth Nova Scotia 1974"

Christopher Allworth

A trained musician, Christopher Allworth became interested in historic musical instruments in the late 1960s. After completing a master's programme in medieval religious music at the University of Illinois, he continued his education at Oxford from 1968 to 1971. His study of the religious iconography and music of the Middle Ages drew him naturally to study the instruments of that period. After returning to Canada, Allworth taught music in Yarmouth, Nova Scotia. In 1984, he moved to Halifax, where he teaches only part-time at the Atlantic School of Theology in order to devote more time to the craft of luthier. He also works as organist and music director at St. John's Anglican church.

The first instruments that Christopher Allworth crafted were reproductions of instruments used before 1450. They include the psaltery, vithele, medieval viol, symphonia (medieval hurdy-gurdy), harp, and lyra (or *gigue*). In the last few years, he has worked exclusively on bow instruments: the viol, the vithele and the lyra. His wife, Carolyn, paints the decorative motifs in tempera and applies gold leaf, in keeping with the style appropriate to each instrument.

Renaissance Instruments

Opus 5 – Lute

The lute could be found throughout Europe by the late Middle Ages. Its Arab precursor, the *ud*, was introduced into Spain by Moorish invaders between 711 and 1492. "Lute" is derived from the Arab word and its article, *al-'ud*. The lute was one of the major instruments in Europe until the late eighteenth century.

During its history, the lute underwent a number of changes. The strings were originally made of gut and mounted in pairs, or courses. Gradually, string quality improved, and the number of strings increased, thereby broadening the lute's range and repertoire. The Renaissance lute had between six and ten courses; this meant from eleven to nineteen strings, as there was usually a single first string. At that time, the lute became a solo instrument, with a repertoire that demanded considerable virtuosity. It frequently accompanied song and appeared in almost all musical ensembles, along with recorders, viols and, somewhat later, the harpsichord.

The belly of this lute is made of alternating strips of maple and rosewood. An Arab-style rose carved in the wood graces the soundboard. The neck and peg box are made of beech, painted black to simulate ebony; the fingerboard is of rosewood; the strings and knotted frets of gut; and the body frets of ivory.

The label is a reproduction of an engraving from the workshop of a luthier published in Paris in 1785, in *Art du faiseur d'instruments de musique et lutherie*.

David Miller

It was during a stay in Halifax on an acting engagement that David Miller had his first experience as a luthier: he made an Appalachian dulcimer from an instruction manual. He subsequently broadened his theoretical knowledge through books and built a variety of instruments, including lutes, guitars and Appalachian dulcimers. When working on early instruments, Miller strives to reproduce as

This Arab-style rose has a distinctive geometric pattern.

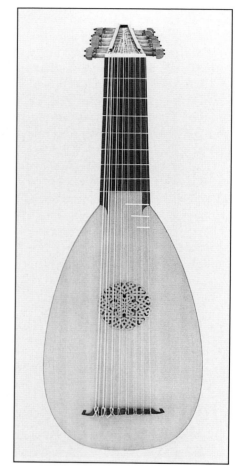

OPUS 5

Lute
By David Miller
Saskatoon, Saskatchewan
1979–80
Maple, spruce, rosewood, beech, pearwood, ivory, ebony, gut
Body: 51 x 29 x 14 cm; neck: 25 cm; peg box: 22.5 cm
CCFCS 85-726
Gift of the Massey Foundation
Label: "David G. Miller Saskatoon, Canada #807"

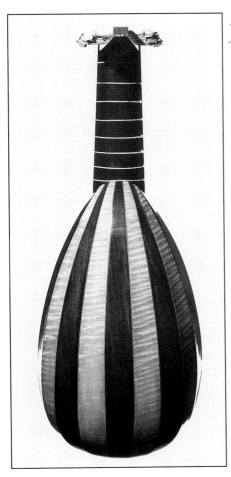

Alternating strips of maple and rosewood form a pleasing contrast.

faithfully as possible their particular acoustic qualities and visual aesthetics. He takes a bit more freedom in crafting traditional instruments, by creating new ornamental motifs or by altering certain technical features in order to improve the instrument.

Opus 6 – Flute

The flute is apparently of Byzantine origin and seems to have been introduced in Germany before spreading to the rest of Europe. Until the fourteenth century, the instrument was played mainly in the Rhine region; it was thus occasionally dubbed the "German flute" after it began to be used in other parts of Europe. During the Renaissance, the flute was still a simple cylindrical pipe with six holes and could be of three different sizes. Period paintings often depict the flautist next to a singer, accompanied by a lute, viol or harp.

Opus 7 – Cornett

The cornett, which became popular in Europe in the early sixteenth century, consists of a leather-covered wooden pipe with six holes on the front and one hole on the opposite side. The instrument

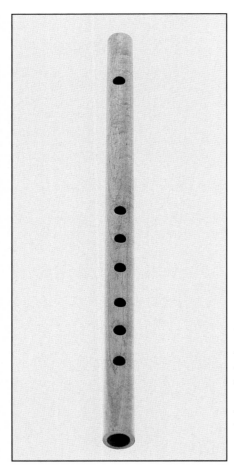

OPUS 6

Flute
By Harry Bloomfield
Montréal, Quebec
Circa 1982
Maple
46.5 cm
CCFCS 85-743.1-2
Gift of the Massey Foundation

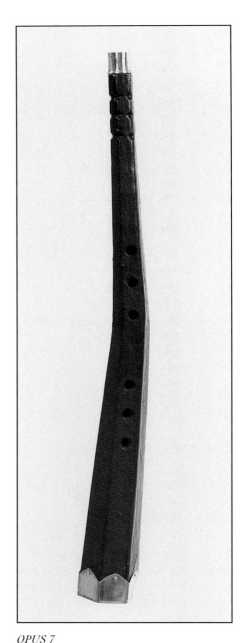

OPUS 7

Cornett
By Edward Eames
Qualicum Beach, British Columbia
Circa 1965
Wood, leather, brass
54 cm
CCFCS 73-1016

originated in the Middle Ages and, as can be seen in illustrations from that era, it was made of a curved section of wild goat horn.

In the sixteenth century, cornetts played a vital role in professional music and often performed with *sackbuts* (precursors of the trombone) in accompanying choirs. This combination was popular until the eighteenth century. However, a seventeenth-century Italian painting shows the unusual combination of a cornett with a violin and a lute.

The cornett shown here is based on an illustration in *European Musical Instruments* by Frank Harrison and Joan Rimmer, which shows a cornettino, itself a reproduction of a sixteenth-century instrument made in 1963 in England.

Edward Eames

Edward Eames received his musical training in England, in particular as a member of military bands while studying at various military colleges. A graduate in music education, he immigrated to Canada in 1953 and settled in British Columbia to pursue a teaching career. His taste for military music sparked an interest in the early instruments used in brass and wind bands. He began building replicas of wind instruments in order to teach their use to his students and to satisfy his own curiosity. Over the years, he built a dozen historic wind instruments and a few stringed and percussion instruments. In 1973, the National Museum of Man (now the Canadian Museum of Civilization) acquired a number of his works.

Opus 8 – Recorder in G

Born in 1492, Sylvestro Ganassi was an active musician, equally accomplished on the viola da gamba and the recorder. Connected with the court of the Doges in Venice, he also performed in Saint Mark's Basilica. In 1535, he published an exhaustive recorder method entitled *Opera Intitulata Fontegara*, which reflects the highly advanced technique of recorder players of the period and the prominent place that the instrument occupied in the music world.

Jean-Luc Boudreau's recorder is a replica of an instrument that was popular at the time Ganassi wrote his recorder method. An innovative combination of a typical Quebec wood with an Italian Renaissance style, the instrument consists of two sections held together with a brass mount. It is tuned to A=440.

OPUS 8

Recorder in G
In the manner of Sylvestro Ganassi
By Jean-Luc Boudreau
Montréal, Quebec
1990
Quebec sugar maple, brass
45 cm
CCFCS 90-507.1-4
Die-stamped marking: "Jean-Luc Boudreau
Montréal 151090"

Jean-Luc Boudreau

Jean-Luc Boudreau has been making recorders and baroque and classical flutes for ten years. Shortly after obtaining a music degree in performance, with a specialization in early flutes, he began to study flute making on his own. In 1983, he received a scholarship from the ministère des Affaires culturelles du Québec to conduct research in European museums, examine original instruments in major collections and visit master instrument makers.

While basing his flutes on historic models, Boudreau enjoys exploring modern technological methods to facilitate his work and enhance the potential of his instruments. He has thus designed special tools for various steps in the construction process, for example, for drilling holes in the pipes and turning the wood. He designs his instruments on a computer and uses synthetic materials, such as moulded polyester resin instead of ivory, to decorate some instruments or build the body of a flute.

Jean-Luc Boudreau has participated in numerous exhibitions in Europe and the United States and has held many lecture-workshops on the making and maintenance of flutes. His Montréal workshop receives orders from Canada, the United States and Europe. He already has some 450 instruments to his credit.

Jean-Luc Boudreau, crafting a flute, 1991.

Baroque Instruments
Use of Technical Drawings

Opus 9 – Pardessus de Viole

*B*eginning in the late seventeenth century in Europe, the viola da gamba was gradually supplanted by the violoncello, whose robust sound was better suited to the orchestras then appearing. However, the viola da gamba continued to enjoy widespread popularity in France until the end of the eighteenth century, during which the pardessus de viole, which is even smaller than the treble viol, was added to the viol family. The French nobility adopted the instrument enthusiastically. Ladies of the court were delighted with the pardessus de viole, whose small size made it charming and entirely in keeping with the elegance of the era. Moreover, the register of the pardessus enabled it to replace the violin, which women avoided playing as it left unsightly marks on the neck.

Dominik Zuchowicz based this pardessus de viole on an instrument in the Musée du Conservatoire de Paris, itself the work of Nicolas Bertrand (d. 1725), one of the great French luthiers of the period and the "faiseur d'instruments ordinaire de la muzique du Roy" (*The New Grove Dictionary of Musical Instruments*). A sculpted woman's head, covered with gold leaf, graces the neck of this meticulously crafted instrument.

Dominik Zuchowicz

In his Ottawa workshop, Dominik Zuchowicz builds and restores instruments from the viol and violin family, such as the early double bass (or *violone*) and the baroque violin. This artisan began his career as an independent luthier in 1974 after spending four years repairing and restoring instruments in a stringed-instrument workshop in Winnipeg. At first, he focused mainly on instrument repair, but began making more and more instruments, specializing in early models. With the help of a Canada Council grant in 1981, he undertook research in European collections and at the Boston Museum of Fine Arts. While in the United States, he acted as restoration consultant for the Boston Symphony Orchestra's Casedessus collection and for the collection of the period music division of the New England Conservatory of Music in Boston. At the same time, he developed a clientèle of musicians with a keen interest in period music.

OPUS 9

Pardessus de Viole
In the manner of Nicolas Bertrand
By Dominik Zuchowicz
Ottawa, Ontario
1991
British Columbia maple and Sitka spruce,
Gabon ebony, boxwood, bone, gut, silver, gold
leaf, linen and glue, oil varnish
Overall length: 63 cm; body: 51 x 18.6 cm;
ribs: 7.6 cm
CCFCS 92-1
Label: "Dominik Zuchowicz Ottawa 20/12/91
1991"

In 1982, Dominik Zuchowicz returned to Ottawa. His clients include numerous professionals, and his instruments are played in the faculties of music of the Université de Montréal, McGill University, Carleton University, and the University of Western Ontario.

This beautiful carved head covered with gold leaf calls to mind the sumptuous furnishings that baroque musical instruments were designed to complement.

Dominik Zuchowicz, in his Ottawa workshop, 1991.

Opus 10 – Pardessus de Viole Bow

As few bows for the pardessus de viole have survived, they are difficult to reproduce. This bow integrates features from a number of original eighteenth-century French and English bows studied by Philip Davis. It is fluted, and its nut is made of snakewood.

Philip Davis

Philip Davis is a Toronto luthier and bow maker who, in addition to making instruments of the violin family and early stringed instruments, specializes in restoring period instruments. A guitarist by training, he studied sculpture and cabinetmaking at the Ontario College of Art in 1969. When he built a classical guitar as a course project, he discovered an activity that was an ideal blend of his interests.

Through instrument making, Davis has pursued fascinating research on the relationship between the form and function of an object. Between 1975 and 1978, he lived in London, where he studied the construction of period stringed instruments. He received two Canada Council grants and conducted intensive research on major European instrument collections. When he received his second grant in 1983, he studied in Germany for one year with master luthier and bow maker J.J. Schroeder. For the past twelve years, Philip Davis has given a course on stringed-instrument making, which he established at the Ontario College of Art.

Opus 11 – Sopranino Recorder

It is astonishing to think that the recorder fell into disuse in the nineteenth century and that even its name was forgotten. In 1919, Arnold Dolmetsch, an English instrument maker and musicologist, became interested in early music and built his first recorder based on a baroque model that is still extant.

During the baroque period, the recorder was no longer built in a single section as it was during the Renaissance, but in three movable sections. This important change enabled musicians to better tune the instrument by lengthening or shortening it slightly. Because the instrument had shorter sections, instrument makers were able to craft the bore with greater care. This method appears to have been developed

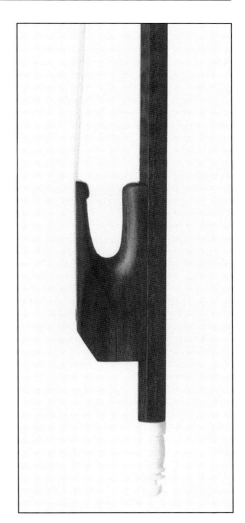

OPUS 10

Pardessus de Viole Bow
By Philip Davis
Toronto, Ontario
1992
Snakewood, bone, horsehair
71.2 cm
CCFCS 92-11

by Jean Hotteterre, a wind-instrument maker in the court of Louis XIV, and was subsequently adopted by the great recorder makers such as Bressan and Stanesby. Thick, elegantly turned ivory mounts on each joint made the recorder highly decorative, a reflection of baroque precepts of beauty.

This instrument is based on a sopranino recorder by Johann Christoph Denner (1655–1707), whose family was noted for its wind instruments. When French recorders consisting of three sections appeared in Germany, Denner took an interest in them and promptly adopted the new construction method. This recorder is in two sections and is tuned to A=415.

Opus 12 – Alto Recorder

Jean-Luc Boudreau based this recorder on an instrument by an eighteenth-century instrument maker named Debey, which is preserved at the University of Utrecht, in Holland. It has three sections, with moulded polyester resin mounts, and is tuned to A=415.

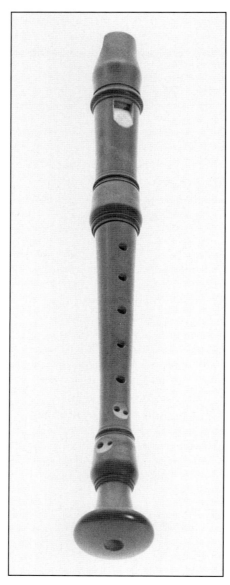

OPUS 11

Sopranino Recorder
In the manner of Johann Christoph Denner
By Jean-Luc Boudreau
Montréal, Quebec
1990
Boxwood, granadilla wood
26.5 cm
CCFCS 90-306.1-3
Die-stamped marking: "Jean-Luc Boudreau
Montréal 190490"

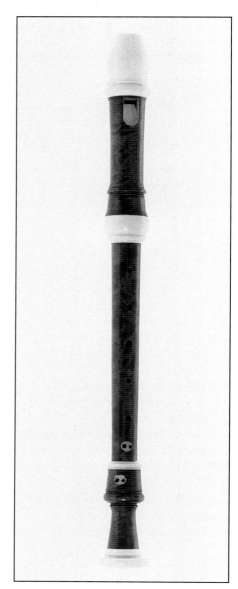

OPUS 12

Alto Recorder
In the manner of Debey
By Jean-Luc Boudreau
Montréal, Quebec
1990–91
Boxwood, moulded polyester resin
50 cm
CCFCS 90-345.1-3
Die-stamped marking: "Jean-Luc Boudreau
Montréal 220790"

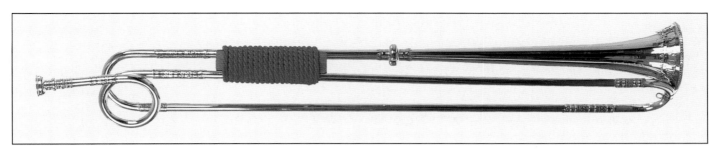

Opus 13 – Baroque Trumpet

For a long time, the trumpet was associated with military life. The trumpet ensembles established by the royal courts and major cities were symbols of strength and wealth. In the seventeenth century, the instrument was added to musical ensembles and eventually acquired a broad repertoire of arrangements by composers such as Corelli, Torelli, D. Gabrielli, Vivaldi and Telemann.

At that time, Nuremberg, Germany, was a leading centre in the manufacture of brass instruments. Metalworking was already a well-established art in the city and, along with the city's prosperity and cultural effervescence, spawned the manufacture of trumpets, trombones and other brass instruments that achieved considerable renown. Baroque trumpets did not have valves; the technical improvements that made the trumpet a chromatic instrument did not appear until the nineteenth century.

OPUS 13

Baroque Trumpet
In the manner of Hanns Hainlein
By Robert Barclay
Gloucester, Ontario
1991
Brass, silver and gold plate
76 cm (excluding the mouthpiece); bell: 9.4 cm
CCFCS 91-118.1-9

The bell of the trumpet is decorated with a garland bearing the maker's name and the place where the instrument was made.

Robert Barclay made this beautiful instrument entirely by hand, based on a drawing of a trumpet by Hanns Hainlein, who belonged to a major family of Nuremberg brass-instrument makers. Dated 1632, the instrument is in the Stadtmuseum in Munich.

This trumpet in D is made of silver-plated brass; the garland and mounts are gold-plated. The bell is decorated with a garland that bears the inscription MACHT ROBT BARCLAI IN OTTW ("Made by Robert Barclay in Ottawa"), emulating the style of Hanns Hainlein, who signed the original trumpet MACHT HANNS HAINLEIN MDCXXXII.

Robert Barclay

Robert Barclay, an arts graduate of the University of Toronto, has been making trumpets for fifteen years. For many years, he taught summer courses in Toronto on brass-instrument making. He is particularly interested in the baroque natural trumpet and is conducting exhaustive research on the celebrated seventeenth- and eighteenth-century Nuremberg trumpets. Several North American and European trumpeters specializing in baroque music own one of his instruments. Barclay has written a number of books on early trumpet-making techniques, including *The Art of the Trumpet-Maker*, published by Oxford University Press. Through his research and the instruments he makes, Robert Barclay actively promotes the revival of the baroque trumpet.

Robert Barclay prepares to cut sheet brass in order to make an instrument, 1991.

Opus 14 – Hurdy-Gurdy

Minstrels, pilgrims and beggars played the hurdy-gurdy, which figured prominently in the secular music of the Middle Ages. Around the fourteenth century, following the Black Plague, the hurdy-gurdy was mainly associated with beggars and blind musicians, and usually held in low esteem. In the eighteenth century, it became the preeminent musical symbol of pastoral life, a reflection of high society's fancy for nature. Writers of that era attempted to ennoble the instrument's origins, just as its appearance was dignified by the addition of mother-of-pearl, ebony and ivory inlays, and sculpted heads. Today, the hurdy-gurdy is used in early-music ensembles or to play traditional music. The instrument is found throughout Europe, including France, Germany, Hungary, Italy, Poland and Scandinavia.

Daniel Thonon based this hurdy-gurdy on an eighteenth-century French instrument. The tortoise-shaped body and, in particular, the head evoke the Arab style much favoured at the court, where the fashion was to dress up as a sultan or Persian princess for celebrations.

Following tradition, the luthier glued an inscription inside the keyboard cover: "This hurdy-gurdy, the thirteenth to come out of my workshop, was ordered by the Canadian Museum of Civilization. By sorry coincidence, it was begun and completed at the same time, to the day, as the so-called 'Gulf War,' which is not, however, a tribute to our civilization. One hundred days, twenty-three keys, one friction wheel, forty-six jacks, and thousands of deaths. Daniel Thonon, Saint-Marc-sur-Richelieu, Quebec, February 1991" [translation from French].

Daniel Thonon

Although Daniel Thonon specializes in hurdy-gurdies, he makes other early instruments, such as the rebec, vithele, psaltery, crwth and lute, and also restores all types of stringed instruments, including the harpsichord, pianoforte and clavichord. As a musician and composer-arranger, he is eager to promote awareness of the hurdy-gurdy and its repertoire. In addition to conducting workshops, he is president of the traditional music ensemble "Ad vielle que pourra," and one of the organizers of the "Vielles et cornemuses" festival, an annual event for fans of Quebec, French, Irish and Breton music.

Born in Brussels, Thonon was surrounded by music from an early age as his father was a jazz pianist. He studied the harpsichord at the Geneva Conservatory and the making of harpsichords and early instruments at the Conservatoire de Paris. His interest in medieval music led him to study its origins in Arab-Andalusian music at the Conservatoire de Tlemcen in Algeria. After settling in Quebec in 1977, he continued

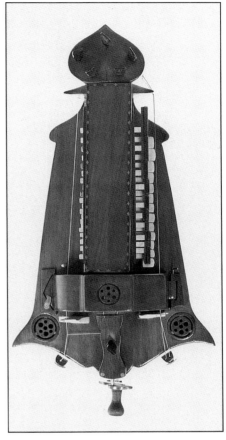

OPUS 14

Hurdy-Gurdy
By Daniel Thonon
Saint-Marc-sur-Richelieu, Quebec
1990–91
Mahogany, amaranth, maple, spruce,
recycled ivory, gut, steel, leather, brass
Overall length (excluding crank)
by width: 70 x 39 cm; sides: 9.3 cm
CCFCS 91-25

to be very musically active and, for some time, was a member of the Claude Gervaise ensemble. To date, Daniel Thonon has made over twenty hurdy-gurdies for a broad range of musicians, including the band Pink Floyd, which owns three of his instruments.

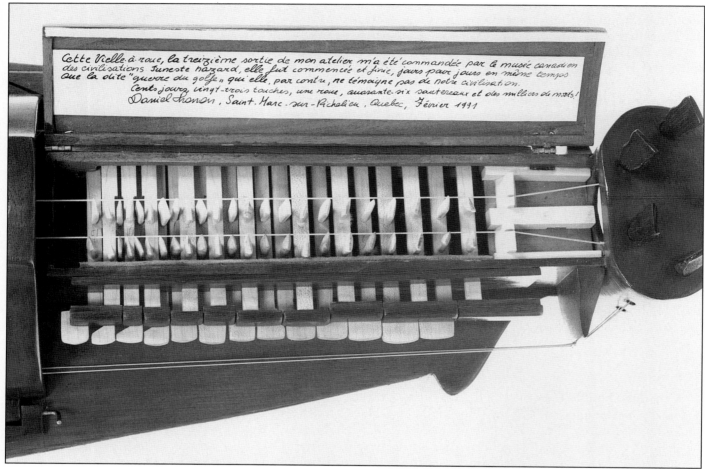

OPUS 14

Close-up view of keyboard, showing label on inside cover.

Close-up view of body and keyboard.

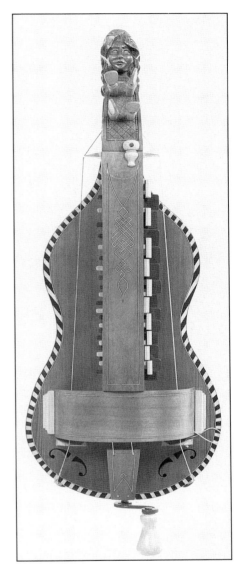

OPUS 15

Hurdy-Gurdy
By Edward R. Turner
Vancouver, British Columbia, 1974
Cherry, redwood, holly, ebony, Eastern maple,
boxwood, brass, steel, gut
Overall length (excluding crank)
by width: 63 x 25 cm; sides: 18 cm
CCFCS 74-1279
Label glued inside the keyboard cover: "Edward
R. Turner, 420 W. Hastings St. Vancouver,
BC, 1974"; "E.R. Turner, Vancouver" is
engraved on the back of the keyboard.

Opus 15 – Hurdy-Gurdy

This hurdy-gurdy is a reproduction of an anonymous eighteenth-century instrument owned by Paul Reichlin of Samstagern, Switzerland. It also resembles an instrument in the collection of the Conservatoire national de Paris made by Pierre Louvet (1711–84), a renowned hurdy-gurdy maker. The guitar-shaped body is made of cherrywood. With its carved head and ebony and holly inlays on the purfling of the body, this instrument is a model of craftsmanship. The strap was woven by Edward Turner.

Substitute Materials

Opus 16 – Baroque Guitar

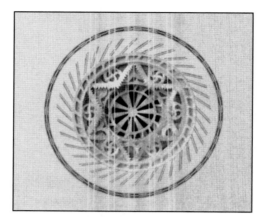

The guitar probably originated in Spain. Guitars with five courses were the most common of the baroque period and came into widespread use in the seventeenth and eighteenth centuries. The baroque guitar differs from the modern guitar not only by the number of its strings, which are made of gut, but also by its smaller size, occasionally curved back, and knotted-gut frets. The rose is surrounded by ornamentation and entirely covered with fine parchment lace. Its special construction and gut strings give the baroque guitar a tone more similar to the lute than the modern guitar.

Inside the parchment rose is a star, consisting of two triangles (one inverted and superimposed on the other), which symbolizes universal harmony.

A repertoire of scholarly music was written for the baroque guitar and played by reputed guitarists in the royal courts. The instrument was also used to accompany songs and traditional music.

A number of celebrated luthiers, such as Antonio Stradivari (1644–1737), made baroque guitars. While these instruments were usually of simple construction, those that survive are often richly ornamented with inlays and marquetry.

Early on in the revival of stringed-instrument making in Canada, Michael Dunn built this replica of a 1641 guitar by René Voboam, which is housed in the collections of the Ashmolean Museum in Oxford. Voboam, a Parisian luthier, was renowned in the seventeenth century for his finely crafted guitars. The back of the original guitar was inlaid with a tortoiseshell chevron motif, which Dunn has reproduced in marquetry. Mounted on the peg box is a piece of ivory bearing the carved inscription "M. Dunn 1974." The Arab rose is made of several layers of delicately cut and gilded parchment. This finely crafted instrument is a tribute to the luthier's outstanding professionalism.

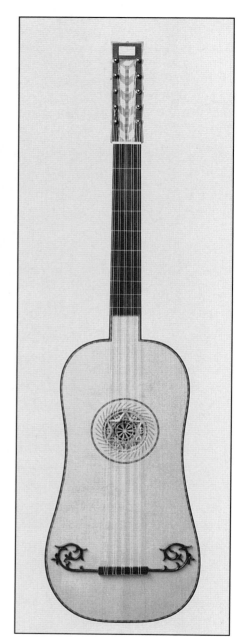

OPUS 16

Baroque Guitar
In the manner of René Voboam
By Michael Dunn
Gibsons, British Columbia
1973
Yew, yellow cedar, German spruce, pine, ebony,
gut, nylon
Overall length: 96 cm; body: 47 x 25 cm;
sides: 9.5 cm
CCFCS 74-158
Label: "Michael Dunn, luthier, made at Gibsons
BC December 1973 #140." The instrument is
also signed by Michael Dunn.

Right: *Marquetry replaces the tortoiseshell*
found on the back of the original instrument.

Michael Dunn

Michael Dunn has been fascinated by the guitar since the age of
eleven, when he learned to play the instrument. He became a versatile
guitarist, conversant with such diverse styles as jazz, folk, flamenco
and bossa nova. In order to study the construction of the guitar, he

undertook a two-year apprenticeship in Palma de Mallorca, Spain, under luthiers Jose Orti and Jose Ferrer. In the early 1970s, Vancouver was the centre of the revival of early music and, like several other luthiers, Dunn became interested in reproducing period instruments. In addition to sharing a workshop with luthier and lutenist Ray Nurse, who taught him to make lutes, he has built harpsichords with Edward Turner.

With over twenty-five years of experience in his craft, Dunn is a leading Canadian luthier. He has built all manner of guitars, from the Renaissance *vihuela* to baroque guitars and acoustic jazz guitars. He has exhibited his instruments extensively in Canada and abroad. In 1980, he was invited to give demonstrations in conjunction with *The Look of Music*, the prestigious exhibition at the Centennial Museum (now the Vancouver Museum). While continuing to build guitars, Dunn teaches a course in stringed-instrument making at Douglas College in Vancouver. He plays with a group whose repertoire is based on the music of Django Reinhardt (who was part of France's Hot Club, a five-man group formed in Paris in 1932). Michael Dunn has built Maccaferri guitars, like those played by the legendary musician, for himself and the other members of his group.

Opus 17 – Alto Recorder

Jean-Luc Boudreau built this recorder on the scale of an instrument by Debey, which is preserved at the University of Utrecht, in Holland. However, although the replica has the same proportions and scale as the original, it is tuned to the modern pitch of A=440, rather than the traditional A=415.

This recorder is made entirely of moulded polyester resin, a synthetic product used as a substitute for ivory. Although the material has many advantages, it is hard to handle as it breaks easily during drilling or turning. Jean-Luc Boudreau has achieved a very modern look to this instrument, whose design complements the construction material.

Opus 18 – Violin Bow

Bow maker Bernard Walke is a biologist by training, and his concern for the environment has led him to question the use of "living" materials, from animal or plant sources, to build musical instruments and other objects. Cow horn offers an interesting alternative to ivory and tortoiseshell, traditional bow-making materials whose use is now banned. The bow shown here is a modern one, with its nut made of cow horn.

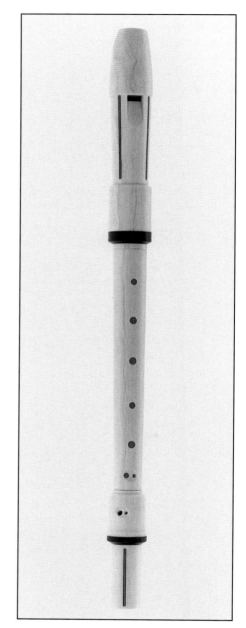

OPUS 17

Alto Recorder
By Jean-Luc Boudreau
Montréal, Quebec
1990–91
Moulded polyester resin
47.7 cm
CCFCS 91-23.1-4

Bernard Walke

Bernard Walke has been a bow maker for ten years. His interest in bow making was sparked by his predilection for classical and Celtic music for violin. But his brother, Gregory, also had a hand in his taking up the profession. In 1974, the two brothers had the opportunity to meet John Doherty, a renowned Irish fiddler, in a Donegal pub. The musician's playing and their sustained contact with Irish and Scottish music encouraged the brothers to take up the violin.

In 1980, back from a stint as a biologist in Nigeria, Walke set about to learn the bow maker's craft, at the insistence of his brother, who had since become a luthier. For two years, Bernard apprenticed under Peter Mach, a luthier and bow maker in Aylmer, Quebec. During this time, he also met Dominik Zuchowicz, who taught him about early music and the construction of viols, which sparked his interest in making baroque bows. He opened a workshop in Toronto in 1982 and studied early French and English bows. In 1984, Bernard Walke settled in Ottawa, where he makes bows for modern violins and for baroque instruments.

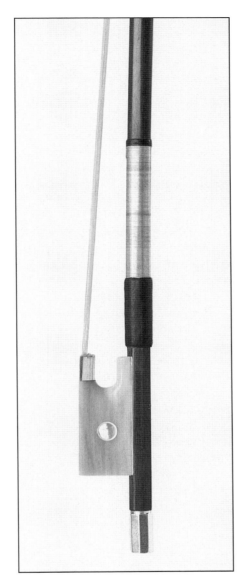

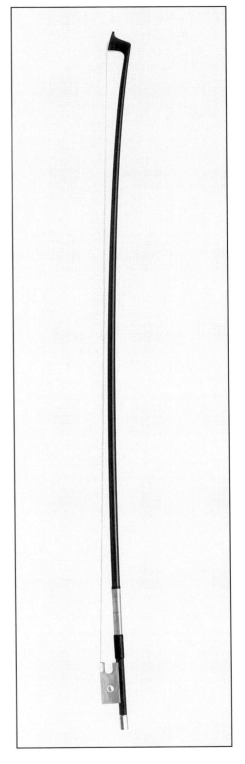

OPUS 18

Violin Bow
In the manner of Dominique Pecatte
By Bernard Walke
Ottawa, Ontario
1991
Pernambuco wood, cow horn, silver thread, silver, mother-of-pearl, abalone, leather, bone, horsehair
74.5 cm
CCFCS 92-15
Brand: "Bernard Walke"

The Jazz Ensemble

Opus 19 – Steel-String Guitar, Archtop and Cutaway

The archtop acoustic guitar owes its invention to the development of the dance orchestras of the 1920s and the big bands of the 1930s. In order to be heard above the brass and percussion sections, the guitar had to be louder. Once again, as a result of musical requirements, the shape of the instrument gradually changed. The arch-top guitar was developed in the Gibson workshops in the United States. John d'Angelico and James d'Aquisto subsequently produced models that were highly favoured by jazz guitarists.

This guitar has many features similar to those of a violin: a curved soundboard, *f*-shaped soundholes and an adjustable bridge over which the steel strings run to the tailpiece, where they are anchored. A steel frame in the neck also helps support the high tension of the strings. Early on in its development, the archtop guitar was equipped with electric pickups, although it cannot match the much more powerful volume of an electric guitar. The instrument has an intimate tone, widely appreciated in the jazz world.

Linda Manzer decorates the fingerboard or peg box of her guitars with inlays, an obvious influence of her first teacher, Jean-Claude Larrivée. This guitar is decorated with motifs representing eight animal species that are endangered or already extinct in Canada. Starting at the peg box, the species are the Dawson caribou, the peregrine falcon, the swift fox, the eastern cougar, the spotted owl, the sea otter, the whooping crane and the bowhead whale. The peg box is ornamented with a floral motif and bears the artist's name carved in a piece of mother-of-pearl. This carefully crafted instrument has a tone worthy of the great jazz guitars.

Linda Manzer

Linda Manzer became interested in making stringed instruments while studying at the Nova Scotia College of Art and Design, where she attended woodworking workshops. She decided to devote herself to the craft and chose as her teacher Jean-Claude

OPUS 19

Steel-String Guitar, Archtop and Cutaway
In the manner of John d'Angelico and James d'Aquisto
By Linda Manzer
Toronto, Ontario
1991
German spruce, maple, mahogany, ebony, abalone, mother-of-pearl, boxwood, bone, steel
Overall length: 104.5 cm;
body: 50.5 x 42.5 cm; sides: 7.5 cm
CCFCS 91-22.1-2

Larrivée, who was working in Toronto. She apprenticed under him for four years, after which she built acoustic guitars for such famous musicians as Pat Metheny, Bruce Cockburn and Milton Nascimento, each of whom owns at least one of her instruments. In 1984, she trained under James d'Aquisto in New York to learn to make archtop guitars in the tradition of John d'Angelico.

Manzer is well known for her innovative spirit, which compels her to never refuse an order, no matter how unusual. For example, she built the celebrated Pikasso 42-string, three-necked guitar for Pat Metheny. In addition to steel-string archtop guitars, Linda Manzer makes classical guitars.

Linda Manzer, in her Toronto workshop, 1991.

Opus 20 – Double Bass

The double bass has changed considerably since the late fifteenth century. It is the lowest-pitched instrument in the orchestra, where its traditional role has been to bolster the bass and rhythm. Moreover, some works call for great virtuosity, for example, Mussorgsky's *Pictures at an Exhibition*, orchestrated by Ravel in 1922. Concertos and sonatas have also been written for solo performances of the double bass. Prominent in jazz, the instrument is usually plucked and imparts great vigour to the rhythm.

Because of the large size of the double bass, the back is normally in two parts. When it is built of a single piece, as it is in this double bass, the wood must come from a tree whose diameter is at least twice the width of the instrument. It should be noted that the luthier generally saws the wood in quarters. When two pieces of wood are used to make the back of the instrument, two adjacent pieces from the same tree are selected and placed side by side to create a pleasing mirror effect.

Peter Mach's reproduction is based on a double bass by George Lewis Panormo which belongs to a member of the Montreal Symphony Orchestra. Panormo (1774–1842) spent his whole life in London, where his father, a luthier of Italian origin, had settled. He built instruments of the violin family as well as bows and guitars.

Mach made this instrument in the late fall and early winter of 1991–92, when the humidity in his workshop was relatively low. Under such conditions, wood releases the moisture that it normally tends to retain; it can reabsorb moisture when ambient humidity increases, without harming the instrument.

Peter Mach

While Peter Mach has always been fascinated by the luthier's art, he was initially trained as a pattern maker in his native Czechoslovakia before turning to instrument making. After immigrating to Canada in 1969, he studied the art under Joseph Kun, a fellow Czech and a luthier and bow maker. In 1976, he enrolled in the international school of stringed-instrument making in Cremona, Italy.

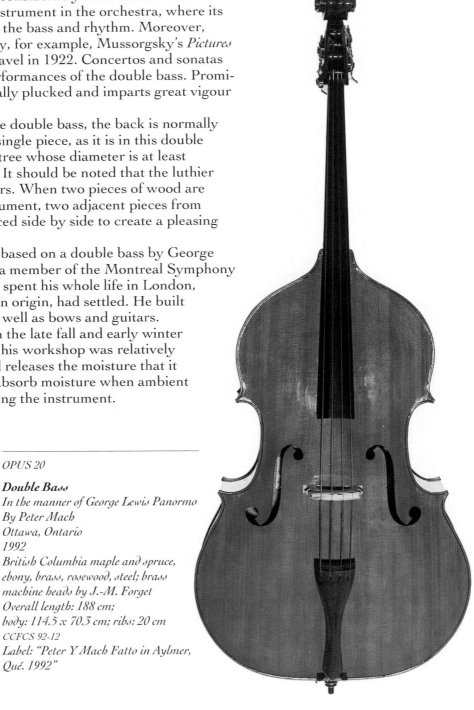

OPUS 20

Double Bass
In the manner of George Lewis Panormo
By Peter Mach
Ottawa, Ontario
1992
British Columbia maple and spruce,
ebony, brass, rosewood, steel; brass
machine heads by J.-M. Forget
Overall length: 188 cm;
body: 114.5 x 70.5 cm; ribs: 20 cm
CCFCS 92-12
Label: "Peter Y Mach Fatto in Aylmer,
Qué. 1992"

OPUS 20

View of back.

After a four-year apprenticeship, he opened his own workshop in Aylmer, Quebec, where he makes and repairs violins and bows. Several musicians in the National Arts Centre Orchestra own instruments by Peter Mach.

Opus 21 – Jazz Drums

In the late nineteenth century, jazz and ragtime flourished, and bass drums, snare drums and cymbals, generally associated with military bands, were adopted to provide rhythm in popular orchestras. Little by little, the percussion section took shape. In the 1920s, drummers borrowed cowbells, woodblocks, cymbals and Chinese tom-toms from the music hall and the circus. Other significant innovations of that time were the Charleston foot pedal and wire brushes for playing the cymbals and the snare drum, which gave more freedom of movement to the drummer.

The development of drum sets is directly linked with that of popular music. Today, jazz drums usually include a small bass drum, several tom-toms mounted above the bass drum and tuned to set pitches, a snare drum, foot cymbals operated with the left foot, cymbals suspended above the bass drum, and a large tom-tom on a low floor stand. This drum set is also used in orchestral performances, of George Gershwin's music, for example, and a variety of film scores by composers such as John T. Williams (of *Star Wars* fame).

The jazz drums shown here were commissioned specially for *Opus*.

Raymond Ayotte

Raymond Ayotte makes drums exclusively to order. Four or five artisans are employed in his workshop, but each drum is individually crafted, thus ensuring complete originality. Ayotte is a professional drummer, who was drawn to drum making through repairing the instruments. He has operated his own workshop since 1983, where he and his colleagues have developed specialized machinery and tools.

Raymond Ayotte has achieved international recognition. Many of his bass and snare drums are owned by symphony orchestras, not to mention jazz and rock musicians who order custom-made drum sets from him. His constant quest for superior quality has led him to develop a drumhead tension-adjustment system and the Ayotte Sensor System, which amplifies the vibraphone.

OPUS 21

Jazz Drums
By Ayotte Drum Company
Vancouver, British Columbia
1991–92
Quebec maple, lacquer, metal, polyester
drumheads
Bass drum: 45 x 40 cm; tom-tom: 35 x 20 cm;
tom-tom: 30 x 22.5 cm; tom-tom: 35 x 35 cm;
snare drum: 35 x 15 cm
CCFCS 92-49.11-19

OPUS 22

Cymbals
By Sabian Ltd
Meductic, New Brunswick
1991
Bronze
Ride cymbals: 52.5 cm;
crash cymbals: 45 cm;
Chinese cymbals: 50 cm;
Hi-Hat cymbals: 35 cm
CCFCS 92-49.1-10

Opus 22 – Cymbals

The practice of striking two metal discs together is very old indeed. Cymbals were used in ancient Mediterranean civilizations. However, cymbals as we know them today originated in seventeenth-century Turkey. Beginning in the eighteenth century, they were used in military bands in Europe; in the nineteenth century, Berlioz introduced them into the symphony orchestra. In the 1920s, they became indispensable to jazz and, somewhat later, to rock music.

Around 1620 in Constantinople, it appears a process was discovered to produce a robust alloy of copper and tin, which made it possible to create a thin, highly resonant disc. The process was handed down from generation to generation in the Zildjian family, whose name means "cymbal maker."

In the late 1920s, some of the family immigrated to the United States, where the encounter between centuries-old expertise and dynamic new music inevitably affected the cymbal's development. As a result, a wide array of cymbals appeared. Nowadays, a drum set can include up to a dozen different cymbals.

The heir of this know-how is the Sabian foundry, where top-of-the-line cymbals are still hammered out by hand, using an age-old technique. The master cymbal maker, Robert Zildjian, is a direct descendant of the family.

Sabian Ltd

Since 1981, the Meductic, New Brunswick, foundry has carried the Sabian name, which is actually an acronym made up of the initial letters of the first names of Robert Zildjian's three children. Robert Zildjian is the owner and president, and a descendant of the Armenian Zildjian family which, for generations, handed down the secret of the alloy used to make cymbals. Robert's father, Avedis, and his great uncle Aram immigrated to the United States at the turn of the century. In 1968, when asked to establish a new branch of the American firm, Robert Zildjian settled in Meductic, a small town he had grown to like after fishing there several times. In 1979, Robert and his brother Armand divided up the company, and Robert became the owner of the Canadian branch. Combining acoustic research and specialized technology with ancestral know-how, Sabian has become a flourishing concern with an international reputation. Its cymbals are exported to all parts of the world.

Like Canadian history, the history of instrument making in Canada is relatively short. We know that one of the first musical instruments was made in colonial times. The Québec cathedral commissioned an organ by sculptor and cabinetmaker Paul Jourdain, who delivered it in 1723. Some one hundred years later, there were a number of established instrument makers, such as Joseph Casavant, a blacksmith by trade and a self-taught organ builder. In 1879, his sons, Samuel and Joseph-Claver, established the Maison Casavant Frères. Among the other instrument makers to achieve prominence in Canada during the nineteenth century was Samuel Russell Warren, who settled in Montréal in 1836 and became the country's first professional organ builder.

As for stringed-instrument making, only in the late eighteenth century is there evidence of the first artisans and restorers. Around 1820, a self-taught luthier, Pierre-Olivier Lyonnais, became the first of four generations to make instruments of the violin family. The Bayeur brothers of Montréal, followed by Camille Couture, also of Montréal, were the first luthiers to establish an international reputation, during the 1920s. The first half of the twentieth century is marked by several outstanding names, for example, George Heinl and George Kindness of Toronto, James Croft of Winnipeg, and Frank Gay of Edmonton.

Piano making began in Québec, thanks mostly to artisans of German and British origins. Frederick Hund was the first piano maker to carry on his trade in the city, in 1816. A number of other piano makers, including Thomas D. Hood, achieved success in the first half of the nineteenth century. In 1851, there were four piano makers in Toronto, ten in Montréal and three in Québec. From the time of Confederation to the turn of the century, several piano manufacturers prospered, including Heintzman, Mason & Risch, R.S. Williams, Willis, and Lesage. However, few of the firms survived the 1930s depression. By 1980, only Heintzman and Lesage pianos were manufactured in Canada.

Instrument making underwent a revival in the late 1960s, in the wake of renewed interest in early music. The movement led to the establishment of musical associations and ensembles, which further encouraged luthiers and other instrument makers. The 1970s were marked by the vitality and know-how of several luthiers, particularly Ray Nurse, Michael Dunn and Edward Turner in Vancouver, Otto Erdész, Jean-Claude Larrivée and Matthew Redsell in Toronto, Antoine Robichaud and Hubert Bédard in Montréal, and Joseph Kun in Ottawa. All these artisans contributed in various ways to the revival of instrument making in Canada.

This section of *Opus* focuses in particular on the making of guitars and instruments in the string quartet, admirably represented by the works of twelve luthiers and four bow makers. As is the case throughout *Opus*, there are occasional references to the European luthiers who inspired the instruments presented here.

Previous page: *Using a penknife, Denis Cormier shapes the soundboard of a stringed instrument, 1991.*

The Guitar

Opus 23 – Classical Guitar

round 1870 in Spain, luthier Antonio de Torres Jurado (1817–1892) began to make guitars almost identical in size and shape to the modern guitar. By the late 1700s, the Spanish luthier Pagès, of Cadiz, had designed guitars which differed increasingly from the baroque instrument: they had six single strings, metal frets instead of gut frets, and experimental fan-shaped bracing under the soundboard. During Torres's lifetime, the guitar began to acquire status as a solo instrument, and the great guitarist Tárrega (1852–1909) paved the way for the modern school of classical guitar. Spurred on by the instrument's growing popularity, Torres built larger guitars and continued to experiment with internal bracing, which gave his instruments a much more robust tone.

The guitar presented here is similar to the flamenco guitar. It is three-quarters the size of a modern classical guitar, like the scaled-down stringed instruments often used by students.

Jim Cameron

Jim Cameron learned to play the guitar in Ottawa and Vancouver. Given his experience in cabinetmaking, he decided one day to construct his own instrument. Encouraged by the results, he went on to build other guitars and, in 1970, opened his workshop in Osgoode, Ontario, where he spent his time crafting stringed instruments.

OPUS 23

Classical Guitar
By Jim Cameron
Osgoode, Ontario
1973
Eastern white cedar, Brazilian rosewood,
Honduran mahogany, Purple Heart,
snakewood, teak, ebony, maple
Overall length: 92.5 cm;
body: 43.3 x 32.7 cm; sides: 9 cm
CCFCS 74-152
Label: "Jim Cameron Osgoode Ont
1973"

OPUS 24

Baroque Guitar
By Michael Dunn and Ray Nurse
Vancouver, British Columbia
1973
Spruce, mansonia, maple, parchment,
ebony, gut, nylon
Overall length: 93.5 cm;
body: 44.5 x 24.5 cm; sides: 8 cm
CCFCS 74-131

The alternating strips of maple and
mansonia on the back are a beautiful
decorative highlight of this baroque guitar.

Opus 24 – Baroque Guitar

This guitar is based on a traditional model; the decorative alternating strips on the back of the instrument probably date it to the early eighteenth century. The Arab-style rose consists of seven superimposed layers of finely cut-out parchment. Carved on a piece of ivory at the base of the neck is the inscription "M. Dunn R. Nurse 1971."

Opus 25 and 26
Steel-String Guitars

These steel-string folk guitars are designed to accompany singing. The fourteen-fret neck appeared in the late 1920s to facilitate the transition from the banjo to the guitar for musicians who played both instruments. Metal-string guitars have existed since the seventeenth century. The modern six-string guitar dates from the mid-nineteenth century, when the famous C.F. Martin company began manufacturing it in the United States.

The instruments shown here represent William Laskin's début as a professional luthier in the 1970s.

William Laskin

William Laskin is an accomplished luthier as well as a guitarist and composer. His numerous activities attest to his great interest in all facets of the luthier's craft. He has organized two major exhibitions on instrument making and has given several talks and demonstration workshops. He is the author of *The World of Musical Instrument Makers: A Guided Tour*, which focuses on instrument makers in the Toronto area, and he is the director of the Associated String Instrument Artisans. In 1971, at the age of eighteen, he met luthier Jean-Claude Larrivée, who agreed to take him on as an apprentice in his workshop. Laskin gave his undivided attention to this new passion and opened his own workshop two years later. To date, he has made over 450 instruments, including acoustic, classical and flamenco guitars, and instruments of the mandolin family. Many of his instruments belong to renowned musicians. William Laskin is also noted for the marquetry and elaborate inlays that adorn his guitars.

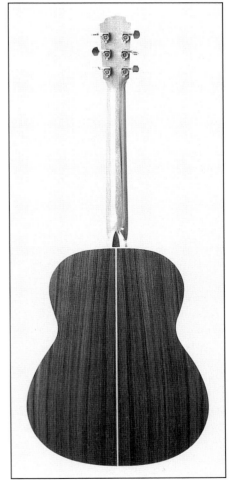

OPUS 25 and 26

Steel-String Guitars
By William Laskin
Toronto, Ontario
1973
Rosewood, cedar, Canadian maple, spruce, abalone, holly, Honduran mahogany, metal, ivory, ebony, steel
Overall length: 103.5 cm; body: 50 x 40 cm; sides: 10.5 cm
CCFCS 74-129.1-2 and 74-130.1-2
Labels: "William Laskin luthier Toronto 73." They are signed "Grit Laskin."

Opus 27
Cutaway Steel-String Guitar

On a cutaway guitar, the soundbox is curved where it meets the neck so that the guitarist's left hand can easily produce the high notes on the fingerboard. Although the cutaway did not become popular until after World War II, it was a distinctive trait of the famous guitars made in the late 1920s by Mario Maccaferri. The first cutaway acoustic guitar, with slightly cutaway side, appears to have been made by the American firm Gibson in 1918. Similar experiments had been carried out on classical guitars in the nineteenth century, but with no permanent results.

This guitar is striking in its beautiful craftsmanship. The decoration on the instrument's neck was inspired by the Grimm fairy tale "Rapunzel." Beautiful Rapunzel's hair cascades down the fingerboard so that her lover can reach her, using the frets. This image is symbolic of the luthier's motto, "Reach for the top." It is magnificently rendered by delicate inlays, which are William Laskin's hallmark.

OPUS 27

Cutaway Steel-String Guitar
By William Laskin
Toronto, Ontario
1991
Spruce, maple, rosewood, ebony
Inlays: abalone, copper, golden
mother-of-pearl, silver, ivory,
maple, ash, walnut, steel
Overall length: 105 cm;
body: 51 x 40.5 cm; sides: 11 cm
CCFCS 91-21.1-2

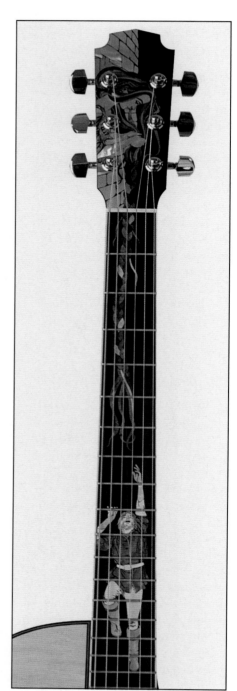

The delicate inlays on the neck of the guitar are a hallmark of William Laskin's work.

Opus 28 – Cutaway Steel-String Guitar

Mario Maccaferri, an Italian born in 1899, was a classical guitarist, luthier and engineer. In the 1920s, he designed and produced for a French firm a prize archtop guitar, noted for its volume. The Maccaferri guitar is associated with the famed guitarist Django Reinhardt. In addition to its characteristic D-shaped soundhole, cutaway side and sophisticated machine heads, the instrument features an interior soundbox, which is designed to resonate and amplify the treble frequencies, or "high end," of the guitar's sound.

Michael Dunn has altered the original Maccaferri design in order to achieve maximum volume and tone. With its shell made of alternating strips of holly and ebony, the guitar can project high frequencies and thus produce greater volume; it is a more "orchestral" instrument, according to Dunn. The machine heads are the Grover Minis type. Like all of Michael Dunn's instruments, this guitar is beautifully crafted. It bears the number 244.

OPUS 28

Cutaway Steel-String Guitar
In the manner of Mario Maccaferri
By Michael Dunn
Vancouver, British Columbia
1991
Western red cedar, Brazilian rosewood, Honduran mahogany, ebony, yellow cedar, sabina, holly, sycamore, brass, steel
Overall length: 101 cm; body: 46.8 x 41 cm; sides: 10.5 cm
CCFCS 91-463.1-3

Michael Dunn, giving a course in stringed-instrument making at Douglas College in Vancouver, 1990.

Opus 29
Cutaway Steel-String Guitar

This guitar is reminiscent of Mario Maccaferri's instruments from the late 1920s, particularly by its D-shaped soundhole and the angle of its cutaway. The adjustable bridge, characteristic of certain archtop guitars, was invented by Lloyd Loar, who worked for the renowned American firm Gibson from 1920 on.

This was Frank Gay's personal guitar.

Frank Gay

Born in Saskatchewan in 1920 to French-speaking parents, Frank Gay was a guitarist and lutenist as well as a composer and luthier. He studied guitar at the New York School of Music and with Norman Chapman in Toronto. A versatile performer, he switched easily from jazz to country, flamenco or classical music. He apprenticed at R.S. William & Co., one of the largest Canadian workshops of the time. In 1953, he opened his own workshop in Edmonton, where he produced prize steel-string acoustic guitars. Country music greats such as Johnny Cash, Don Gibson and Hank Snow have owned his guitars. His instruments have earned the appreciation of distinguished classical guitarists, including Alirio Diaz and Montoya. Gay also built folk and Renaissance guitars, lutes, mandolins and banjos. Always active in the music world, in 1959 he established a classical guitar association, one of the first in the Canadian west. Frank Gay is recognized as an innovative artisan and a major figure in the history of Canadian stringed-instrument making.

Opus 30 – Flamenco Guitar

Unlike the classical guitar, the flamenco guitar often uses the traditional wooden pegs, and the strings are much closer to the frets in order to facilitate quick passages. It is lighter than the classical guitar so that it can be held almost vertically on the right thigh of the flamenco guitarist.

OPUS 29

Cutaway Steel-String Guitar
By Frank Gay
Edmonton, Alberta
1972
Spruce, rosewood, Honduran mahogany, chrome-plated steel, ivory, mother-of-pearl, ebony, steel
Overall length: 98.3 cm;
body: 47 x 41.5 cm; sides: 10.4 cm
CCFCS 91-554
Label: "Frank Gay Custom Made Guitars 10718, 97 Street Edmonton Alberta Model MCB 1972 FGK 1772"

The rose on this instrument was designed and crafted by the luthier. A piece of carved ivory graces the bridge. The back of the guitar is in three sections.

Oskar Graf

Born in Germany in 1944, Oskar Graf learned cabinet-making, and furniture and commercial design in Berlin. After immigrating to Canada in 1968, he became interested in making stringed instruments and, in 1970, began to construct simple instruments associated with traditional music, such as the Appalachian dulcimer and, later, the banjo, box zither and mandolin-banjo. He made his first classical and steel-string guitars in 1973 and added lutes to his repertoire in 1980. Graf also repaired and restored instruments while living in Kingston from 1982 to 1985.

Graf approached instrument making through cabinetmaking, an art with many comparable features. He pursued his apprenticeship as a luthier by visiting European museums and the workshops of celebrated luthiers and by partici-pating in workshops given by European masters, such as José Romallinos. Oskar Graf's work-shop is located in Clarendon, Ontario.

OPUS 30

Flamenco Guitar
By Oskar Graf
Clarendon, Ontario
1981
Cherry, cedar, ebony, Indian rosewood,
mother-of-pearl, ivory, nylon
Overall length: 99.5 cm;
body: 48.5 x 36.5 cm; sides: 9.5 cm
CCFCS 83-766
Gift of the Massey Foundation
Label: "Oskar Graf '81 Clarendon
Ontario." The instrument is also signed
"Oskar Graf."

The back of the guitar is made of three sections.

Opus 31 – Cutaway Steel-String Guitar

This Cutaway Presentation guitar designed by Jean-Claude Larrivée is similar to his Larrivée Body model. The lower bouts are slightly wider and the sides slightly narrower than on the "Dreadnought" guitar. Built for the *Opus* exhibition, this instrument has a powerful, well-balanced sound and features original inlays.

Jean-Claude Larrivée

A native of Montréal, Jean-Claude Larrivée studied guitar at the Royal Conservatory of Music of Toronto in the mid-1960s and learned the luthier's craft under Edgar Münch. After five-and-a-half years of intermittent apprenticeship, including a stint in New York working with Manuel Valasquez, Larrivée opened his own workshop in Toronto in 1968. From that time on, he built around thirty guitars a year and significantly influenced the development of guitar making in Toronto. A number of his apprentices are now respected luthiers, with a reputation for fine craftsmanship. Larrivée moved to Victoria in 1977 and then to North Vancouver in the early 1980s, where he established his current workshop.

After visiting a number of assembly-line instrument workshops and studying quality control methods, Larrivée organized his workshops with a view to boosting output. Twelve employees work entirely by hand, producing instruments which Larrivée is convinced are of superior quality. In his view, workers who specialize in one phase of production become better than anybody else at what they do. Jean-Claude Larrivée's clients include many Europeans, Japanese and Australians, and famous guitarists like Bruce Cockburn and Eugene Martynec.

OPUS 31

Cutaway Steel-String Guitar
By Jean-Claude Larrivée
North Vancouver, British Columbia
1991
British Columbia spruce, Indian rosewood and ebony, Honduran mahogany, steel
Inlays: abalone, mother-of-pearl, silver
Overall length: 103.3 cm;
body: 50.5 x 40.5 cm; sides: 11 cm
CCFCS 92-14.1-2

Opus 32 – Classical Guitar

The Passacaille model is noted for its elegant shape and the refined materials used in its construction. Neil Hebert has played up the beauty of the maple's light wood by contrasting it with ornamental ebony purfling. The soundboard is made of spruce; the cast-bronze machine heads are by I. Sloane.

Over the years, various features of the classical guitar have been standardized, although a number of luthiers continue to improve the instrument's construction. Neil Hebert's guitars display certain distinctive characteristics, such as the bracing of the soundboard and the shape of the bridge, which the artisan has designed to achieve a particular tone and enhance the overall construction.

Neil Hebert

Montréal luthier Neil Hebert has specialized in making classical guitars for over fifteen years. An engineer by training, he blends the luthier's art with the rigour of science. Using special software, he conducts spectrographic analyses of his guitars in order to determine acoustic qualities. His interest in instrument making stems basically from a love of music, which led him to study the guitar for several years. But Hebert was also prompted to make instruments by a natural attraction to manual work and by a certain frustration at not finding

OPUS 32

Classical Guitar
By Neil Hebert
Montréal, Quebec
1991
British Columbia spruce, Canadian curly maple, ebony, bronze, nylon
Overall length: 99.5 cm; body: 48 x 36.8 cm; sides: 9.5 cm
CCFCS 91-544
Label: "Neil Hebert Montreal no 166 1989."
The instrument is also signed "Neil Hebert."

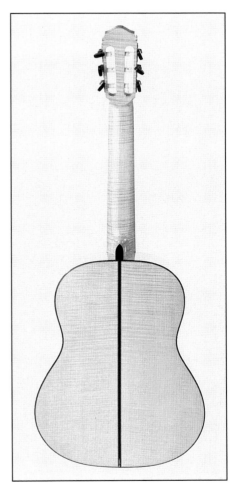

The luthier used only indigenous woods, except for the ebony, which plays up the beauty of the light maple.

an instrument he liked. A self-taught luthier, he has worked professionally at instrument making since 1975. To date, he has made approximately 160 guitars for professional musicians in Europe and North America. Neil Hebert has given workshops at the École de Lutherie Artistique du Noroît, in Québec, with a focus on guitar making, acoustics, and the use of computers in instrument making.

Ivo Loerakker, outside his workshop in Saint-Barthélemy, 1990.

The String Quartet

Opus 33 – Violin

The violin achieved its present shape in the sixteenth century and quickly gained popularity by the end of the century. However, violin making flourished in particular between 1650 and 1750 in Cremona, in northern Italy, where Stradivari and other famous luthiers crafted their instruments. In the late eighteenth and early nineteenth centuries, the violin underwent changes that enhanced its power and brilliance, making it a leading instrument in increasingly larger concert halls. The neck was elongated, inserted in the top-block, and tilted. Moreover, the fingerboard was elongated, the bridge heightened, and the tail-piece braced. Another innovation was the chin rest. All these changes enabled more vigorous striking and bowing, in addition to improving the resistance of the strings to pressure from the bow. Despite these modifications in the construction of the instrument, the violin's body has remained unchanged.

This meticulously crafted violin is based on a Stradivari model. The varnish is light amber, and the scroll, peg box and purfling are outlined in black.

OPUS 33

Violin
In the manner of Antonio Stradivari
By Ivo Loerakker
Saint-Barthélemy, Quebec
1991
Tyrolean fir, spruce,
Yugoslavian maple, steel
Overall length: 58.5 cm;
body: 35.2 x 20.4 cm; ribs: 3.1 cm
CCFCS 91-451
Label: "Ivo Johannes Loerakker fecit
St-Barthélemy, Québec A.D. 1991"

View of back.

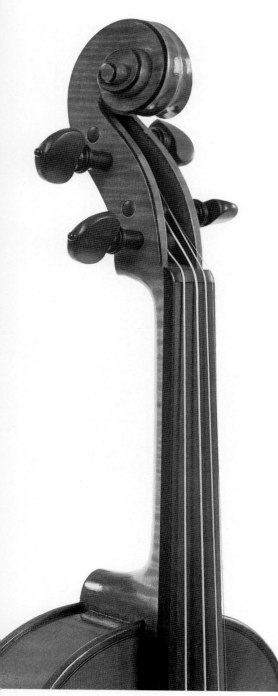

Ivo Loerakker

Born in Haarlem, Holland, Ivo Loerakker is the son of a luthier and was thus introduced to instrument making at a very early age; he made his first violin when he was eleven. In 1974, after graduating from the prestigious school of instrument making in Mittenwald, Germany, Loerakker was invited to work with Claude Fougerolle in Montréal. Three years later, he opened his own workshop, where he repaired and made violins, violas and violoncellos. In 1982, he moved his workshop to Saint-Barthélemy, where he has worked since. Ivo Loerakker is a member of the American Federation of Violin and Bow Makers.

The scroll on a violin has the same proportions as those on classical Greek Ionic columns.

Opus 34 – Violin

Bartolomeo Giuseppe Guarneri (1698–1744), known as Giuseppe del Gesù, was the last and most celebrated member of a family of Cremona luthiers. His violins are unquestionably as renowned as those of Stradivari. Guarneri was no doubt influenced by his countryman, as he was by the distinguished instrument makers of Brescia, whose instruments combined the two great traditions of Italian baroque stringed instruments. He was nicknamed "del Gesù" because of the labels that appear on his violins, bearing the monogram *IHS* (*Jesu Hominum Salvator*) and a Roman cross.

John Newton

Toronto-area luthier John Newton has been crafting instruments full-time for ten years. His manual skill was developed, he says, by building reduced scale models and by drawing. Newton began to play the violin when he was around fifteen, and his love of music for stringed instruments eventually drew him to instrument making. After building five violins on his own, he vowed to become a professional luthier. He apprenticed under Otto Erdész, a Romanian-born luthier and master viola maker who had settled in Canada after living in New York for seventeen years. In the course of his apprenticeship, Newton learned all facets of stringed-instrument making, from wood selection, design and varnishing to final adjustment.

Newton made several violas under Erdész's direction and became his assistant. In 1981, he received a Canada Council grant that enabled him to continue his studies and launch his career as a professional luthier. To date, he has made approximately one hundred instruments, which are widely appreciated by professional musicians and are played in major orchestras such as the Toronto Symphony, the Canadian Opera Company Orchestra, and the Amadeus Ensemble. Newton says that he is fascinated and inspired by the demands of his craft: balancing manual dexterity and musical understanding with artistic expression; respecting an ancient tradition while meeting the practical needs of contemporary musicians; and achieving consistent quality while bearing in mind the numerous variables inherent in natural materials.

Opus 35 – Viola

The viola has rarely enjoyed the same esteem as the violin, although composers have, over the years, gradually discovered the richness of its tone, at once veiled and warm, sombre and velvety.

OPUS 34

Violin
In the manner of Giuseppe Guarneri
By John Newton
Desboro, Ontario
1991
Maple, spruce, steel
Overall length: 59 cm;
body: 35.5 x 20 cm; ribs: 3 cm
CCFCS 92-13.1-2

The violin owes its brilliance to the perfect ratio between its tessitura and dimensions. If applied to the viola, this ratio would yield an instrument too large and difficult to play. By "cheating" a bit on the ratio, the luthier obtains an instrument with structural and acoustic imperfections, but with a unique tone and character.

Developed in northern Italy, the viola was already a well-established member of the violin family by about 1535. It was used to play the middle parts in musical ensembles, usually to round out the harmony. It was not until the mid-eighteenth century that it came into its own as a solo instrument.

The viola plays an important role in chamber music, especially in string quartets. With Haydn, Mozart and Beethoven, the quartet achieved a perfection that elevated it to the leading genre in classical chamber music. As chamber music developed, the four instruments in the string quartet acquired equal importance, with the viola and violoncello becoming as prominent as the two violins. When Mozart and Haydn organized informal quartets with their colleagues Dittersdorf and Vanhal, the viola was played by Mozart.

David Prentice

In 1980, violinist David Prentice was shopping for a better violin but was put off by the price. He decided then and there to embark upon the adventure of instrument making. The manual nature of the work, he confides, brought back the childhood thrill of building scale models and playing with Meccano sets. He sought the necessary information on violin making in books but found them rather perplexing. However, he met luthier Joseph Curtin, who proved extremely helpful. Prentice made his first violin in a course given by luthier Philip Davis at the Ontario College of Art, and was so satisfied with his first instrument that he decided to pursue a career in the field.

Initially, Prentice made both violins and violas, with the help and advice of John Newton and Joseph Curtin. But he later specialized in violas, whose dimensions and design, less standard than those of the violin, allowed him more freedom. Building one instrument at a time, he has found in his daily work a balance between the technical and the sculptural and creative facets of his art. His clients include advanced students and professional musicians, and his instruments appear in symphony orchestras and string quartets across Canada and the United States. In 1990, he received a Canada Council grant.

"The most fascinating aspect of instrument making for me is sound," says David Prentice. "How to achieve a consistently good quality of sound, how to maximize power, how to achieve different tonal colours: these are questions that rely on so many variables from

OPUS 35

Viola
In the manner of the Brescia school
By David Prentice
Flesherton, Ontario
1991
Ontario maple, spruce, steel, ebony
Overall length: 68 cm;
body: 41 x 24.5 cm; ribs: 3.8 cm
CCFCS 92-9.1-2

quality of wood to arching, to varnishing and set-up. This sound element raises the craft of instrument making from high-quality woodworking to an art: the art of sound production."

Opus 36 – Violoncello

Like the other members of the violin family, the violoncello was developed in northern Italy (Cremona, Brescia, Bologna and Milan) by numerous luthiers, including Andrea Amati, Gasparo da Salo, Andrea Guarneri and Francesco Ruggeri. The instrument appeared early in the sixteenth century, although the term "violoncello" came into use a full century later, to replace "bass violin."

Usually, the construction of an instrument changes simultaneously with its musical role. The violoncello became a solo instrument in the late seventeenth century, when sonatas and concertos were written for it. In the late eighteenth century, Boccherini, a composer and virtuoso cellist, featured the instrument in his works and concerts.

Jean-Benoît Stensland's beautifully crafted violoncello, based on Antonio Stradivari's Piatti model, is finished with a reddish brown varnish on gilded background.

Jean-Benoît Stensland

Jean-Benoît Stensland has had thorough training as a luthier. He began his apprenticeship in Montréal in 1976 under luthier Jules Saint-Michel and later under Antoine Robichaud. After acquiring the basics of instrument making, he worked at Peate Musical Supplies in Montréal, where he learned how to restore all types of stringed

OPUS 36

Violoncello
In the manner of Antonio Stradivari's Piatti model
By Jean-Benoît Stensland
Montréal, Quebec
1992
Yugoslavian maple, Tyrolean fir, ebony, steel
Overall length: 122.5 cm; body: 76 x 44.5 cm; ribs: 12.5 cm
CCFCS 92-46
Label: "J.B. Stensland Luthier Montréal 1991"

instruments. This training enabled him to obtain a Canada Council grant in 1980 to study for four years at the international school of stringed-instrument making in Cremona, Italy. After graduating in 1984, he earned a certificate of merit for one of his violins in the international instrument-making competition of the Violin Society of America. Back in Canada, Stensland opened a workshop with luthier Thérèse Girard. Together, they have developed techniques based on the Italian and French schools, striving for a particular ideal tone while focusing on the visual aesthetics of the instrument.

To date, Jean-Benoît Stensland has made approximately sixty instruments, some of which are played by members of the Montreal Symphony Orchestra, I Musici de Montréal, and the Orchestre métropolitain.

Opus 37 – Violin Bow

The bow, although often overshadowed by the stringed instrument it accompanies, is as complex to make as the instrument itself. In fact, bow making is an art, just like instrument making.

While its exact origin is uncertain, the bow appears to have come from central Asia. A tenth-century treatise by a Baghdad theoretician and scholar named Al-Faradi on the *rebab*

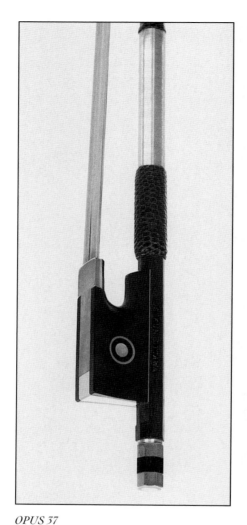

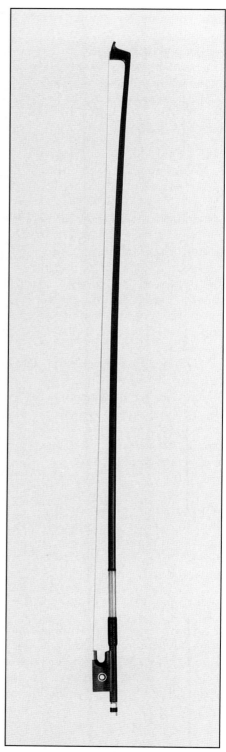

OPUS 37

Violin Bow
By Joseph Kun
Ottawa, Ontario
Circa 1982
Pernambuco wood, ebony, silver,
mother-of-pearl, leather, horsehair
74.5 cm
CCFCS 83-720
Gift of the Massey Foundation
Brand: "Jos Kun Ottawa"

(Arab violin) proves that the bow already existed by then. Moreover, around this time the bow was introduced into Europe from the Arab and Byzantine countries.

The modern bow, developed in the mid-eighteenth century, differed from its predecessors in its slightly concave curve, making it stronger and more precise. Around 1780, the Parisian bow maker François Tourte (1747–1835) developed the bow which, except for minor variations, is still used today.

The hair of the bow is horsehair—as many as two hundred strands on a modern bow. To ensure that the horsehairs adhere properly to the strings, they are rubbed with a solid resin called colophane or arcanson, which is obtained by distilling turpentine.

The bow featured here has an octagonal stick, decorated with silver thread. The ebony nut is ornamented with mother-of-pearl and silver, and the head plate is made of silver.

Joseph Kun

Joseph Kun learned instrument making in his native Czechoslovakia. Since settling in Canada in 1968, he has earned an international reputation for his bow making. A luthier as well as a bow maker, he crafts violins, violas and violoncellos, and is also well known for his repair and restoration work. Guarneris, Stradivaris and other valuable instruments are often sent to his workshop for delicate repairs. Joseph Kun is a member of the American Federation of Violin and Bow Makers. His bows have won numerous awards in international bow-making competitions.

Opus 38 – Violin Bow

This is a fine example of a French bow in the manner of François Tourte. The stick is octagonal, and the head plate is covered with walrus ivory. The nut is ornamented with mother-of-pearl and silver, and the adjusting screw is made of silver.

Reid Hudson

A native of Toronto, Reid Hudson studied the double bass before turning to bow making. He apprenticed under the celebrated Ottawa bow maker Joseph Kun in the mid-1970s and opened his own work-shop in 1977. Since 1980, he has lived on Vancouver Island, where he continues to practise his art. He has received numerous first prizes for the quality of his bows in American and Canadian competitions. Reid Hudson serves on the selection jury for Canada Council grants to luthiers and other instrument makers.

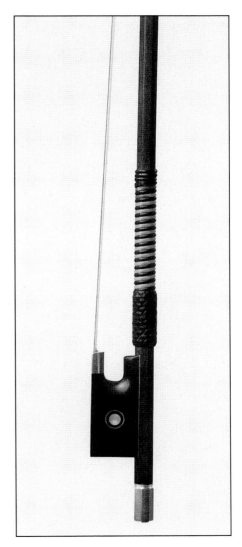

OPUS 38

Violin Bow
In the manner of François Tourte
By Reid Hudson
Duncan, British Columbia
1990
Pernambuco wood, silver, horsehair, walrus ivory, mother-of-pearl, ebony, synthetic whalebone, snakeskin
74.6 cm
CCFCS 90-496
Die-stamped marking: "Reid Hudson"

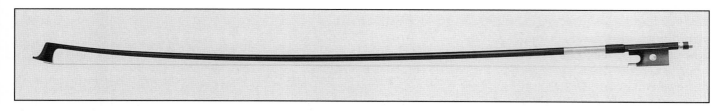

Opus 39 – Viola Bow

This bow was designed for luthier David Prentice's viola. The stick is round, and the adjusting screw is made of ebony and silver. The ebony nut is ornamented with a mother-of-pearl eye.

François Malo

A cellist by training, François Malo cites his curiosity as a musician as the reason for his entry into the world of bow making. After studying for a year in Québec with the Strasbourg bow maker Yves Matter, he decided to broaden his knowledge in France. Finding a teacher in the closed community of bow makers is no mean feat. However, with his bows tucked resolutely under his arm, François Malo managed to convince more than one master bow maker to accept him as an apprentice. He obtained three Canada Council grants which enabled him to study with Gilles Duhaut in Mirecourt (the French capital of stringed-instrument making), William Salchow in New York, and the renowned Stéphane Thomachot in Paris. To date, François Malo has made nearly three hundred bows. His clients include musicians from major Canadian and American orchestras, in Toronto, Montréal, Winnipeg, New York, Philadelphia and Cleveland, to name but a few.

Opus 40 – Violoncello Bow

The style and decoration of this bow are Thérèse Girard's unique design. A striking feature is the superb silverwork on the nut and the adjusting screw.

Thérèse Girard

A trained violist, Thérèse Girard apprenticed as a luthier under Jules Saint-Michel in Montréal. She trained for three years in his workshop, where she made her first violin. In 1980, she received a Canada Council grant to attend the four-year program at the international school of stringed-instrument making in Cremona, Italy. There, she learned to make instruments of the violin family, including baroque instruments, and studied restoration, the production and application of varnishes, the history of stringed-instrument making, and the different schools of luthiers. While in Italy, she also took a

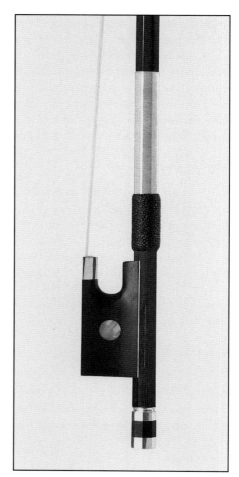

OPUS 39

Viola Bow
By François Malo
Montréal, Quebec
1992
Pernambuco wood, ebony, silver,
mother-of-pearl, bone, leather, horsehair
75 cm
CCFCS 92-16
Brand: "F Malo à Montréal"

two-year course in bow making.
In addition to making and
restoring modern and baroque
bows, Thérèse Girard specializes
in the engraving of nuts and
screws, a technique learned from
a master jeweller. After returning
to Montréal in 1984, she opened
a workshop, where she col-
laborates with Jean-Benoît
Stensland. Their clients include
professional musicians, soloists
and advanced students in various
orchestras and faculties of music
in the Montréal area and beyond.

OPUS 40

Violoncello Bow
By Thérèse Girard
Montréal, Quebec
1991
Pernambuco wood, ebony, mother-of-
pearl, silver, silver thread, ivory,
snakeskin, horsehair
72 cm
CCFCS 92-45

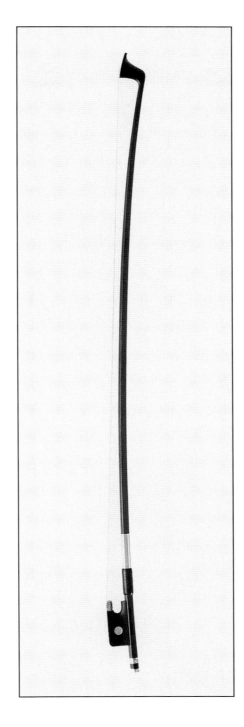

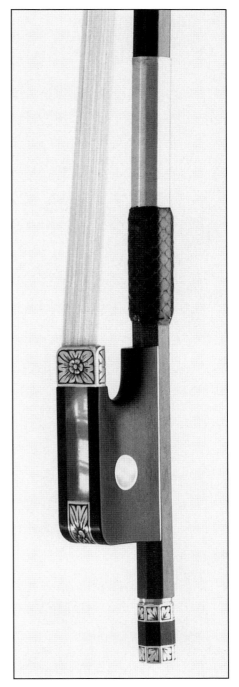

The Flute

Opus 41 – Baroque Flute

There were great strides in the making of flutes during the baroque period. Beginning in the late seventeenth century, the instrument was built in three sections; it acquired a key, and the bore became cylindrical and conical. Like the recorder, the flute was probably transformed by the Hotteterre family, French instrument makers in the court of Louis XIV. The modifications made it possible for instrument makers to drill the bore with greater accuracy and for musicians to tune the instrument.

The eighteenth century marked an important period in the development of the flute. The instrument was made in four sections, or joints, and keys were added. These joints were built in different lengths so that performers could tune the flute to the standard pitches of particular cities or to those used in chamber, church or opera music. In this century of transition between the baroque and classical periods, the flute gained widespread popularity. Virtuoso performers gave public concerts, a novelty that subsequently became common practice.

Peter Noy

Peter Noy has been making flutes for over ten years. In his Toronto workshop, opened in 1988, he specializes in making recorders and early flutes, and repairs modern woodwind instruments.

A flautist and devotee of early music, Noy was prompted by curiosity to explore flute making and teach himself the craft. He undertook research by studying the construction of various early instruments and acquired solid experience in repairing wind instruments by working for Gary Armstrong Woodwinds. A number of grants from the Canada Council and the Ontario Arts Council enabled him to study historic instruments in a dozen European collections.

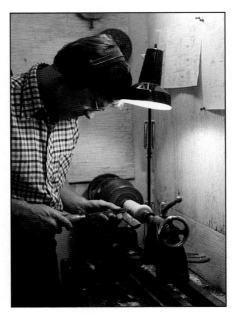

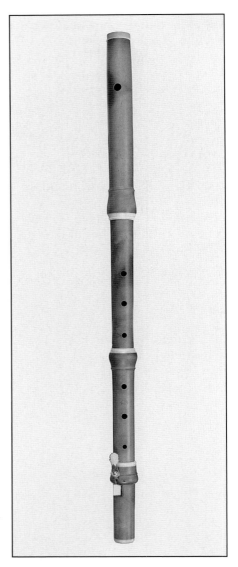

OPUS 41

Baroque Flute
In the manner of Jacob Denner
By Peter Noy
Toronto, Ontario
1992
Boxwood, bone, silver
62.3 cm
CCFCS 92-136
Brand: Artist's seal, followed by "Noy."

Peter Noy, working at the lathe.

Peter Noy has participated in numerous exhibitions and international shows in North America and Europe.

Opus 42 – Baroque Flute

Jean-François Beaudin based this flute on an instrument by Johann Joachim Quantz (1697–1773), which is part of the Miller Collection in the Library of Congress in Washington. A German flautist, composer and theoretician, Quantz taught the flute to Frederick the Great, among others. His treatise on the flute, *Versuch einer Anweisung die Flöte traversiere zu spielen* ("On playing the transverse flute"), published in 1752 in Berlin, is one of the most extensive sources of information on the instrumental practice of that time. Quantz's flutes differed from Hotteterre's earlier models: they were made in four sections, had a second key, and were equipped with an internal slide between the head and middle joints so that the pitch could be lowered without unbalancing the tuning.

Whereas Quantz's flute has six interchangeable joints, Jean-François Beaudin decided to reproduce the joint with a pitch of A=392, which was the most frequently played, as suggested by the wear on the holes. Beaudin also substituted plastic mounts for the ivory mounts on the original flute. The instrument maker's name is inscribed in a curve, often seen on baroque instruments, above a turtledove with open wings. Jean-François Beaudin identifies with the turtledove, which he feels symbolizes freedom; its introspective song is gentle but far-reaching and hauntingly mysterious, like the music of the baroque flute.

Jean-François Beaudin

Musician and flute maker Jean-François Beaudin specializes in seventeenth- and eighteenth-century music. His virtuosity on the baroque flute and the recorder was developed at the Royal Conservatory of Music in The Hague. At this renowned school he was also introduced, by Australian instrument maker Frederick Morgan, to flute making and the art of drafting plans of early flutes. Thanks to three grants from the ministère des Affaires culturelles du Québec, Beaudin undertook a number of training stints and trips to examine collections of early instruments in order to study them and prepare inventories and plans. In addition to producing technical drawings for his own research, Beaudin has been commissioned to produce more than fifty technical drawings of instruments for the Musée instrumental du Conservatoire national supérieur de musique in Paris, the University of Edinburgh's Collection of Historic Musical Instruments, and the Musikinstrumenten-Museum des Staatlichen Instituts für Musikforschung in Berlin. With a solid fifteen years' experience at his craft, Jean-François Beaudin has made over one hundred

OPUS 42

Baroque Flute
In the manner of Johann Joachim Quantz
By Jean-François Beaudin
Frelighsburg, Quebec
1992
Ebony, silver, plastic, brass, cork
67.3 cm
CCFCS 92-134
Die-stamped markings: "BEAUDIN"
(above a turtledove); "1992"; "111"

instruments, including several flutes and recorders as well as flageolets, mainly for European clients. During a recent trip to India, he developed an interest in the Indian bamboo flute.

Jean-François Beaudin checks the tuning on a flute, 1992.

Opus 43 – Classical Flute in C

The development of the wooden flute reached its peak in the latter half of the eighteenth century. A group of London flute makers had apparently developed a flute with four keys. Other pairs of keys were subsequently added, bringing the total to eight.

Mozart, Beethoven and Schubert wrote music for this type of flute, which was usually made of wood, but occasionally of ivory, and was equipped with up to eight keys. It was not until the mid-nineteenth century that the metal flute appeared, thanks to the German flute maker Theobald Boehm (1794–1881).

The flute shown here is based on a model by Richard Potter (1726–1806), an English flute maker who significantly improved the construction of the instrument. This flute in C with six keys (C#, D, D#, F, G# and Bb) has an interchangeable middle joint so that the instrument can be tuned to A=430 and A=440. It is made of granadilla wood and has polyester resin mounts. The keys are made of brass.

Opus 44
Butterfly Headjoint for Flute

An instrument is rarely created from scratch; it is usually the product of a long process and extensive experimentation. However, the invention of the modern flute is often attributed to a single man, Theobald Boehm (1794–1881), a German

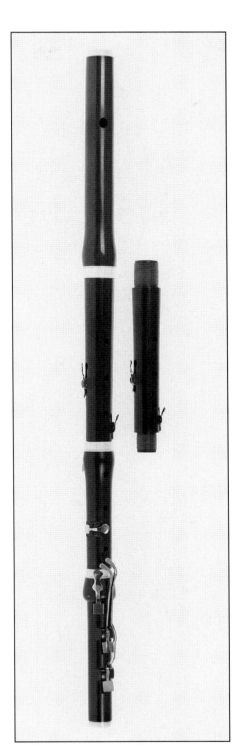

OPUS 43

Classical Flute in C
In the manner of Richard Potter
By Jean-Luc Boudreau
Montréal, Quebec
1990–91
Granadilla wood, moulded
polyester resin, brass
65.8 cm (or 66.8 cm with
interchangeable joint)
CCFCS 91-24.1-6
Die-stamped marking: "Jean-Luc
Boudreau Montréal 610690"

goldsmith, flute maker and professional flautist. Boehm redesigned the location and size of the tone-holes to increase the instrument's volume, and designed the complex mechanism that allows the keys to operate independently as well as interact with others in different combinations. He also used metal instead of wood for the revamped flute, which he completed in 1847.

Despite its powerful volume, which must certainly have been appreciated at a time when there was constant striving for greater brilliance, Boehm's flute gained ground rather slowly because the innovative key mechanism required new fingering techniques. For this reason, wooden flutes were still found occasionally in orchestras in the early twentieth century.

No matter how sophisticated the instrument, there always seems to be room for research and improvement. This flute headjoint with Butterfly embouchure wall and lip plate, designed by Jack Goosman, is considered by many flautists to be a breakthrough in flute making because it appreciably alters the flow of air, which enters the flute more rapidly. The silver headjoint is engraved "J.P. Goosman Toronto," followed by the monogram "JPG" and "CAN.PAT. 1,275,837."

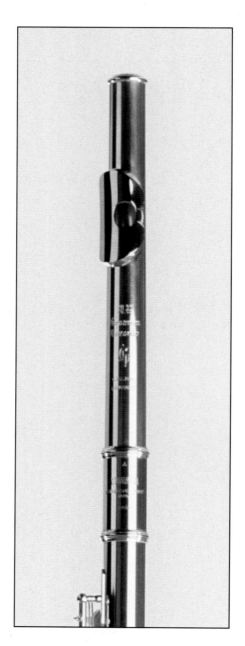

OPUS 44

Butterfly Headjoint for Flute
By J.P. Goosman Flutes Ltd
Pickering, Ontario
1991-92
Sterling silver headjoint with
14-carat gold embouchure
22.3 cm
CCFCS 91-560

Jack Goosman

Before becoming a flute maker, Jack Goosman studied the flute under some famous teachers. In 1968, he obtained a performance degree from Duquesne University, in Pittsburgh, and began work in the reputable Boston workshop of Verne Q. Powell Flutes Inc. This company, which helped make Boston the centre of American flute making, had introduced the French-style flute to the United States before developing its own model. It was in this workshop that Goosman, who had previously concentrated on flute repair, discovered he had a genuine talent for flute making.

In the spring of 1971, Goosman opened his own workshop outside Toronto. The move was doubly beneficial: for the Toronto area, which had few if any flute makers; and for Goosman, who was fond of this part of the country, where he had spent his summers as a child. By 1974, his repair workshop was doing very well, and he set about making flutes, with the help of his wife Mara, also a flautist, and his assistant Yutaka Chiba. One of Goosman's first flutes was for Nicholas Fiore, principal flautist in the Toronto Symphony.

The high quality of Goosman's instruments quickly earned him an enviable reputation. His clients include such well-known flautists as James Galway, Jeanne Baxtresser and Robert Cram, to name but a few, and symphony orchestra flautists from Europe, Japan and North America. In 1989, Goosman devoted part of his time to research and design the Butterfly headjoint and embouchure. Patented in Canada and the United States, the Butterfly headjoint enables the flautist to articulate notes more quickly and accurately. It extends the upper register of the alto flute and increases its volume. The Butterfly headjoint was unveiled at the 1989 National Flute Association Convention in New Orleans. Currently, Jack Goosman works full-time at producing the headjoint, while Mara Goosman manages the workshop.

The Marimba

The marimba is an ancient instrument, found in central Africa and the Malay Archipelago, where it took the form of a small xylophone with calabashes placed under the bars to act as resonators. It later appeared in South and Central America, where it was made by African slaves. European settlers modified the marimba and added carefully tuned resonators. Another feature of Central American marimbas is the resonators outfitted with mirlitons, which give the instrument its characteristic nasal timbre. These membrane-mirlitons attached to the resonators are typical of early Mexican marimbas.

Around 1910, the marimba made its appearance in the percussion section of Western orchestras. Wooden resonators were replaced by metallic tubes that could be tuned by moving metal discs located in their lower extremity, and the mirlitons were eliminated.

OPUS 45

Marimba
By Denis Grenier
Cap-de-la-Madeleine, Quebec
1992
Sugar maple, kingwood, Honduran
rosewood, aluminum, steel, rubber, nylon
Length: 170.5 cm; width: 76 cm;
height: 88 cm
CCFCS 92-50

Opus 45 – Marimba

The frame of this marimba is made of sugar maple and kingwood, covered with black lacquer and decorated in purple and gold. Locking casters make the instrument easier to move. The tubular resonators have a gold lacquer, and the Honduran rosewood bars are finished in satin lacquer. This marimba has a range of fifty-two notes—four octaves plus a minor third. It was built specially for *Opus*.

Denis Grenier

Denis Grenier is one of the few North American instrument makers to specialize in percussion bar instruments. He became interested in the craft while repairing school instruments. Through hours spent dismantling and reassembling numerous instruments, he became thoroughly familiar with their construction and developed an eye for identifying their design flaws and qualities. When he received his first order, he decided to design his own prototype. As a self-taught artisan, Grenier has eagerly sought the advice of cabinetmakers, engineers and musicians. His father, a certified machinist, has also been a valuable resource person.

Grenier opened his workshop in 1982 and gave up teaching percussion music in 1987 to concentrate full-time on instrument making. While most of his instruments are designed for the educational sector—post-secondary institutions, universities and conservatories— his clients also include professional percussionists from various musical ensembles. Denis Grenier has developed approximately fifty exclusive models of instruments, for which he has devised the design, acoustic calculations, and assembly procedures.

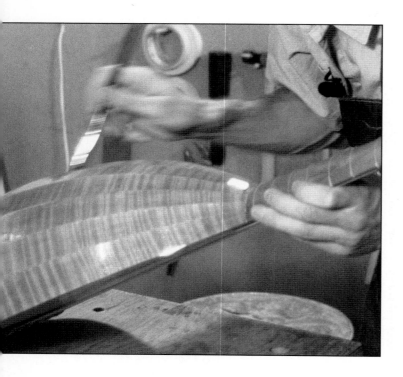

The beauty of a musical instrument—apart from its sound—does not stem from a few aspects of its decoration, but from the balance of its proportions. "What's good for the eye is good for the ear" has guided luthiers and other instrument makers for centuries in their quest for perfection.

In the three hundred some years between the beginning of the Renaissance and the end of the baroque period, there was a broad array of musical styles. Changes were closely linked with history and social conventions, which dictated the kinds of art objects people preferred at different periods. For example, the Italian Renaissance, with its humanist approach inherited from the Greeks, encouraged the production of musical instruments

that, in addition to pleasing the ear, would satisfy and delight the eye, like painting and architecture.

This philosophy also spawned the belief that "Man is the measure" in the rule of proportions. Vitruvius (Marcus Vitruvius Pollio), a Roman architect employed by the emperor Augustus, conveyed this notion in *De Architectura*, which explains that the human body and its extended limbs mark the confines of a perfect circle and a square. This rule of proportions, called "the golden mean," was illustrated by numerous Renaissance artists, the most famous of whom was undoubtedly Leonardo da Vinci (see *The Vitruvian Man of Perfect Proportions*).

Studies on the proportions of Renaissance and baroque musical instruments suggest that luthiers of those periods were aware of the mathematical concept of the golden mean. Its application to instrument making produced shapes which are considered aesthetically perfect and which, on closer study, reveal the geometry of the instrument.

Previous page: *Grant Tomlinson, applying varnish to the back of a Renaissance lute in Vancouver, 1991.*

Above: *Detail.*

This geometry provided the luthier with a simple method to achieve a harmonious shape.

During the baroque period, this sober and somewhat abstract aestheticism coexisted with a decorative style so exuberant that it sometimes overwhelmed the true function of musical instruments, which came to symbolize social standing.

Yet, the practice of decorating musical instruments is very old indeed. Some decorated instruments have been found to date back to the Stone Age and the Bronze Age in ancient Egypt and ancient Greece. In the Middle Ages, the decoration of the psaltery led to the tradition of rose decorations found on later stringed instruments. The organ, associated with religious music, was decorated with sculptures that blended with the architecture of its site. In secular music, some instruments began to be embellished; for example, the hurdy-gurdy was given a sculpted head. This decorative practice continued in the centuries that followed, reaching its peak in the baroque period. Decorative styles subsequently became more subdued, confined to details such as roses on soundboards, sculpted heads, and marquetry.

With the advent of the industrial era and mass production, instrumental decorations gradually disappeared. By the turn of the century, hand-decorated instruments had all but vanished. The practice was revived only later, with the renewed interest in early music and instruments produced in the "historically correct" manner. Today, the instruments played in symphony orchestras are quite sober. The focus is mainly on the instrument's tone, along with its harmonious shape, pleasing colour, fine craftsmanship and, for the musician playing it, balance and personal suitability.

The Trio Sonata

Opus 46 – Baroque Violin

As discussed under Opus 33, the baroque violin (prior to the 1800s) differed from the modern violin. It had a smaller bass bar and soundpost, and its neck, which was not inserted in the topblock, was only slightly tilted. The bevelled fingerboard and the tailpiece were decorated with marquetry. Today, the G string and sometimes the D string of the baroque violin are made of gut wound with wire; but the other strings are all gut.

The instrument seen here is based on a late baroque model, like those made in Mozart's time. The ribs, scroll and back are made of a single piece of European curly maple; the two-piece soundboard is made of European spruce. The flecked reddish-orange varnish has been applied in varying hues. The neck and tailpiece are inlaid with boxwood; and the nut and saddle are made of ivory, the fingerboard of ebony-covered maple, the pegs of ebony, and the endpin of polyester.

Denis Cormier

Born into a family of fiddlers, Denis Cormier was exposed to the violin from an early age. Focusing on classical-violin making, he apprenticed under Frédéric Boyer in Paris for two years and also trained under the Dutch master Willem Bouman in The Hague. After returning to Montréal, he opened a workshop in 1980. What he builds, says Cormier, is a sound. This sound is, in fact, a special one: his modern and baroque violins are played by professional musicians in Canada, the United States, Europe and Japan. Denis Cormier has made a number of instruments for the Orchestre symphonique de Montréal, the Orchestre métropolitain, the Studio de musique ancienne, and the group I Musici.

Opus 47 – Baroque Oboe in C

While double-reed instruments have existed for a long time, the direct ancestor of the modern oboe originated in the seventeenth century. The baroque oboe appears to have been developed in France by instrument makers in the Hotteterre family, who introduced it to the court of Louis XIV in 1657. The new instrument produced the same volume as the ancient *chalumeau* but was also capable of soft tones. It quickly gained favour throughout Europe and became one of the most expressive instruments in the orchestra. Beginning in the nineteenth century, the oboe gradually underwent changes, such as the addition of a key mechanism, which led to the modern oboe.

OPUS 46

Baroque Violin
By Denis Cormier
Montréal, Quebec
1991
European curly maple, European spruce, boxwood, ebony, gut, ivory, polyester
Overall length: 59 cm; body: 35.2 x 20.5 cm; ribs: 3 cm
CCFCS 91-543
Label: "Denis Cormier fait à Montréal en 1991 No. 103"

This oboe is based on an instrument by Johann Christoph Denner that is preserved in Nuremberg, Germany. The Denners were renowned wind-instrument makers in that city. Four such oboes are still extant. This instrument in C has three brass keys and is tuned to A=415. To produce a sharp note, the musician simply covers one of the double holes and leaves the other open. Nitric acid was used to produce the instrument's colour.

Martin Léveillé

A graduate in oboe and chamber music from the Conservatoire de musique de Québec, Martin Léveillé specializes in repairing and making wind instruments. Thanks to grants from the ministère des Affaires culturelles du Québec and the Canada Council, in 1983 he undertook a two-year practicum in the workshops of Jean Mignot in Paris, where he learned to make modern oboes under Michel Viger and Gérard Mignot. In 1986, he continued his studies in Utrecht, Holland, where he made baroque oboes under Toshi Masegawa. He also trained under Guy Dupin in Zurich, focusing this time on the repair of modern oboes. Since his return to Montréal, in addition to repairing modern oboes, he has crafted ten baroque oboes. He works closely with a number of luthiers and other instrument makers to design and produce instrument parts and specialized tools for making stringed instruments. Since 1991, Martin Léveillé has collaborated with Jean-Luc Boudreau to make baroque oboes.

Opus 48 – Harpsichord

Although the shape and keyboard of the harpsichord are similar to those of the piano, the two instruments are very different from each other, with vastly different timbres. The strings of the piano are struck whereas those of the harpsichord are plucked. Each key on the harpsichord activates a jack connected to a plectrum that plucks the string.

The earliest evidence of an instrument of this type is from 1397, when a Paduan lawyer wrote that Hermann Poll claimed to have invented the *clavicembalum*. As of the late fifteenth century, the harpsichord is depicted in a number of paintings and described in several manuscripts, in particular that of Henri Arnault de Zwolle (see section entitled "Making Musical Instruments"). The harpsichord became more widely used in Europe, acquiring a particular character in each country. Italy, Flanders, France, Germany and England all had great harpsichord makers, and numerous schools of harpsichord making coexisted until the late eighteenth century, when the instrument was supplanted by the *pianoforte*. This new instrument, whose strings are struck, made it possible to play with varying nuances—hence its

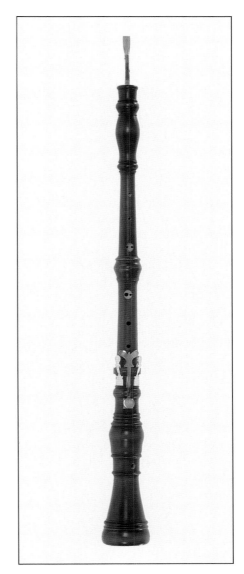

OPUS 47

Baroque Oboe in C
In the manner of Johann Christoph Denner
By Martin Léveillé and Jean-Luc Boudreau
Montréal, Quebec
1991
Boxwood, brass
57 cm
CCFCS 91-420.1-4
Die-stamped marking:
"Boudreau Léveillé Montréal"

Italian name meaning "soft-loud"—in keeping with the musical tastes of the day. The harpsichord did not come back into use until the late nineteenth century, when a Parisian named Érard built the first modern harpsichord, with a quite different sound from that of the seventeenth- and eighteenth-century instruments. Since 1945, there has been a return to the construction and sound of early harpsichords.

Yves Beaupré based this harpsichord on two Flemish instruments, one by Joseph Joannes Couchet, dated 1679, the original of which is in the Smithsonian Institution, and the other by Joannes Ruckers, dated 1640, preserved at Yale University.

Couchet was related to the Ruckers family of Antwerp, who dominated the Flemish school between the sixteenth and eighteenth centuries. Their

OPUS 48

Harpsichord
In the manner of J.J. Couchet
and J. Ruckers
By Yves Beaupré
Montréal, Quebec
1991
Black cherry, Sitka spruce, bone, ebony, linden, tempera, brass
Length: 193 cm; width of keyboard: 78.7 cm; thickness: 24.1 cm
CCFCS 91-2.1-11
Inscription on nameplate: "YVES BEAUPRAE ME FECIT MONTREALAE MCMXCI." On the pin block, the instrument is signed "Y.B. no 64."

The soundboard, painted by Danièle Forget, displays a foliage motif, tulips, a parakeet, a dragonfly and bees —all characteristic of Flemish ornamental style.

instruments, which influenced harpsichord makers throughout Europe, are highly regarded by contemporary instrument makers, who strive to reproduce their tone.

This instrument has a single keyboard of fifty-two keys and two eight-foot unison registers. It is tuned to a short octave, and its range is GG/BB-d'''; a transposing keyboard allows the shift in pitch from A=415 to A=440. The soundboard, signed "Danièle Forget 1991," is decorated with a bronze rose and tempera motifs consisting of flowers, insects, parakeets and berries. Forget has added the indigenous Canadian ephemera to the insects traditionally painted on Flemish harpsichords. The decoration of the body is typical of Flemish instruments: marbling on the sides and block-printed paper on the inside of the lid.

Yves Beaupré

Yves Beaupré is a Montréal instrument maker who has established a solid reputation in the realm of early music. A graduate in harpsichord performance from the Université de Montréal, he made his first instrument on his own. Since this first experience in 1976, he has devoted himself to instrument making and now has sixty harpsichords to his credit. A Canada Council grant in 1981 enabled him to study major collections of instruments in Europe and meet master harpsichord makers.

While Beaupré follows traditional instrument-making techniques, he prepares his own technical drawings, convinced that understanding and interpreting the principles of early harpsichord making is artistically and musically preferable to slavish copying. He has thus brought some innovations to the instruments, making them more mechanically reliable and stable. The National Arts Centre in Ottawa owns a Beaupré harpsichord, as do numerous internationally renowned professional harpsichordists.

Opus 49 – Bass Viol

The viola da gamba achieved prominence during the Renaissance and the baroque period. In the late fifteenth century, Spanish musicians apparently attempted to play the *vihuela* (a type of guitar) with a bow. From this experience was born the viol, which the Italians of the sixteenth century dubbed the viola

OPUS 49

Bass Viol
In the manner of Richard Meares
By Ray Nurse
North Vancouver, British Columbia
1991
British Columbia maple and Sitka spruce,
ebony, ivory, gut
Overall length: 121.5 cm;
body: 66 x 36.5 cm; ribs: 12 cm
CCFCS 91-419
Label: "Ray Nurse 1991 Vancouver Canada
no 914"

da gamba because it was held between the legs. They thus distinguished it from instruments in the violin family, which they designated as *viola da braccio* ("arm-viol"). Promoted by court musicians, the instrument rapidly gained favour in Germany, France and England.

Like a number of other Renaissance instruments, the viol comes in several different sizes, the most common being the treble, tenor and bass viols. As viols harmonize very well together in ensembles, an extensive repertoire of works was written for them, especially in England. Such ensembles, called consorts, were made up of professional and upper-class amateur musicians.

During the baroque period, the bass viol was more widely used than the others. It commonly provided continuo accompaniment to the harpsichord in chamber music.

Ray Nurse built this bass viol in the manner of an instrument by Richard Meares that is preserved in the Victoria and Albert Museum. Meares worked in London during the second half of the seventeenth century, at a time when the trio sonata had just been introduced in England. As viol making reached a peak of refinement, the pure lines of the instruments were embellished with limited decoration.

This is the type of viol, with sloping upper bouts and strikingly elegant lines, that Ray Nurse built for *Opus*. The peg box is covered with intertwining leaves carved in relief. The scroll consists of a magnificent open

As the carving of the scroll is not limited by the same acoustic considerations as the other parts of the instrument, it allows the luthier a greater margin for artistic expression.

Notice the motifs created by the decorative purfling.

shell, carved from one side to the other. The purfling traces a geometric design on the back and a floral motif on the soundboard. The varnish is a light colour. The luthier's name appears on the bridge of this six-string instrument.

Ray Nurse

Ray Nurse teaches the lute in the Music Department of the University of British Columbia and is internationally recognized as one of North America's foremost luthiers. He began his career in instrument making in 1965. In 1967, he became an apprentice to Ian Harwood and John Isaacs in England while studying the lute under Dianna Poulton. Since then, he has thoroughly researched the construction of the lute and other stringed instruments in European and North American museums. Nurse helped found the Vancouver Early Music Society and has been involved in establishing early-music ensembles.

Since 1976, Nurse has been a director of the Lute Society of America and has given numerous talks and workshops on lute performance and making. In the early 1970s, he opened a workshop in Vancouver, where he builds replicas of historic instruments as faithfully as possible to the methods and aesthetics of early luthiers. Ray Nurse's lutes are admired by world-famous professional musicians.

Opus 50 – Baroque Violin Bow

While there were many types of bows in the Middle Ages, they commonly had an arched stick. However, the baroque bow was almost straight. At that time, a screw system, similar to the one used on modern bows, was introduced to adjust the tension of the hair. While the baroque bow does not enable the musician to achieve the same technical prowess as with the modern bow, it was nevertheless suited to the music of its time, particularly chamber music, which required little volume.

The nut and adjusting screw on this baroque violin bow, which is based on an eighteenth-century French model, are made of fossilized walrus ivory. Designed to play a gut-string baroque violin, the bow weighs forty-eight grams.

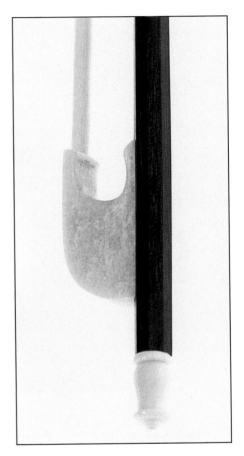

Louis Bégin

While studying the viola da gamba at the Conservatoire royal de Bruxelles, Louis Bégin took woodworking courses to help him relax. His subsequent fascination with blending wood and music eventually led him to bow making. He completed this stay in Europe with a first prize in viola da gamba performance and with several training sessions in bow making to his credit, including a course given by bow maker Gilles Duhaut in Mirecourt, France. Bégin opened his workshop in Montréal in 1981, dividing his time between bow making and teaching the viola da gamba; he has also frequently performed with early-music ensembles. Bégin has returned to Europe a few times to study major collections in instrument museums. Since 1988, he has worked exclusively at bow making. Louis Bégin's baroque and modern bows are sold in Canada and exported mainly to the United States, France, Germany and Japan.

OPUS 50

Baroque Violin Bow
By Louis Bégin
Montréal, Quebec
1990–91
Banyan, fossilized walrus ivory, horsehair
70.5 cm
CCFCS 91-19
Brand: "Louis Bégin" (hidden by the nut),
"180291."

Opus 51 – Bass Viol Bow

The nut and adjusting screw on this pike-head bow, based on a seventeenth-century French model, are made of fossilized walrus ivory; the fluted stick is made of snakewood. The bow, which weighs seventy-six grams, was designed for *Opus* to accompany Ray Nurse's viola da gamba (Opus 49).

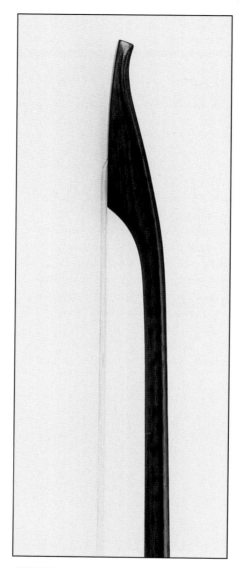

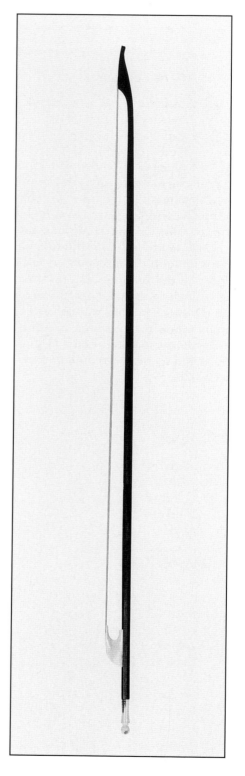

OPUS 51

Bass Viol Bow
By Louis Bégin
Montréal, Quebec
1990–91
Snakewood, fossilized walrus ivory,
horsehair
77 cm
CCFCS 91-18
Die-stamped marking: "Louis Bégin"

The Lute

Opus 52 – Renaissance Lute

This instrument features metal frets instead of the traditional knotted-gut frets of the Renaissance era. When luthiers began to make lutes in the twentieth century, they used metal frets like those on the modern guitar. Moreover, lutenists during the revival of early music were often guitarists, whose playing technique was not geared to the lute.

This lute is typical of instruments built in the early 1970s, when there was a burgeoning interest in early music and instrument making in Canada. Some twenty years later, the same luthier built the instrument labelled Opus 53.

Colin Everett

A native of England, Colin Everett settled in Ottawa when he immigrated to Canada in 1966. He studied guitar at that time, but gradually became interested in the lute. As lutes were difficult to obtain back then, he decided to build one. While Everett now specializes in lute making, his fascination with Renaissance music has also led him to make other instruments of that period, such as the viola da gamba, harpsichord, crumhorn and rackett. He has belonged to several early-music ensembles and performed at numerous concerts and festivals. His instruments, which

OPUS 52

Renaissance Lute
By Colin Everett
Ottawa, Ontario
1974
New Brunswick maple, ebony, British Columbia red cedar, mahogany, metal, nylon
Overall length: 70.6 cm;
body: 47.5 x 52.8 cm; depth: 16.5 cm;
peg box: 25.5 cm
CCFCS 74-692.1-2

include over seventy lutes to date, are played in Canada, especially in Quebec. In addition to pursuing his musical activities, Colin Everett currently teaches chemistry at Algonquin College.

Opus 53 – Renaissance Lute

Based on an instrument by Giovanni Hieber, a German luthier who settled in Venice in the second half of the sixteenth century, this lute has seven courses, or pairs of strings. The body is made of strips of maple, and the soundboard of spruce, embellished by an Arab-style rose carved in the wood. The instrument is sparingly ornamented as the luthier preferred a simple style, more in keeping with the instrument commonly used during the Renaissance. Highly decorated lutes, and those made with rare materials such as ivory, were reserved for the nobility and upper middle classes.

Opus 54 – Renaissance Lute

The model for this lute, which is outfitted with seven courses, is an instrument made by Vuendelio Venere in Padua in 1592 and preserved in the Accademia Filarmonica in Bologna. Venere produced a number of instruments in the late sixteenth and early seventeenth centuries.

Grant Tomlinson crafted this strikingly beautiful replica after conducting painstaking research

OPUS 53

Renaissance Lute
In the manner of Giovanni Hieber
By Colin Everett
Manotick, Ontario
1992
European spruce, New Brunswick maple, African padouk, rosewood, gut, parchment, nylon, plastic
Overall length: 68 cm; body: 44 x 31 cm; depth: 15 cm; peg box: 20.5 cm
CCFCS 92-2.1-2
Brand: "CJE 1992"

OPUS 53

Variations on this Islamic-inspired rose appear on many Renaissance lutes.

OPUS 54

The Gothic-style rose carved on this soundboard resembles delicate embroidery.

in European museums. The body consists of twenty-five strips of yew, separated by thin bands of sycamore. Carved in the spruce soundboard is a delicate gothic-style rose. Tomlinson made his own amber varnish. The design of the bridge, which is made of dyed pearwood, is typical of Paduan luthiers in the late sixteenth century.

Grant Tomlinson

In 1975, Grant Tomlinson's attempts to play early music on the guitar led him to study the lute under Canadian instrument maker and musician Ray Nurse. He soon became interested in making stringed instruments, primarily the lute. Intent on achieving the closest possible reproduction of baroque and Renaissance instruments, Tomlinson conducted intensive research on lutes in major European collections for nearly a year. He measured, photographed and studied over seventy original lutes. In 1986, he received a Canada Council grant to study lute making under the renowned English luthier Stephen Gottlieb.

In addition to making lutes, Tomlinson is active in the Lute Society of America, for which he gives lectures and workshops and writes specialized articles for publication. His reputation now firmly established, Grant Tomlinson attracts a clientèle of professional musicians and serious amateurs from Europe, Japan, the United States and Canada.

The body of this lute consists of twenty-five strips of yew, separated by thin bands of sycamore.

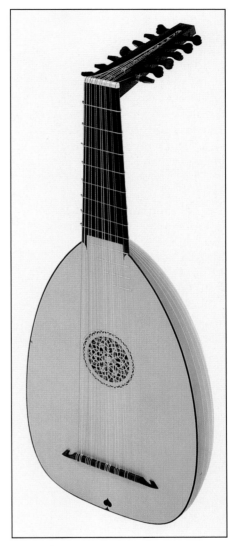

OPUS 54

Renaissance Lute
In the manner of Vuendelio Venere
By Grant Tomlinson
Vancouver, British Columbia
1991
Spruce, yew, sycamore, pearwood, gut, ivory
Overall length: 67 cm; body: 44 x 30 cm;
depth: 14 cm; peg box: 19.7 cm
CCFCS 91-455
Label: "Grant Tomlinson
Vancouver BC 1991."

Opus 55 and 56
Renaissance Soprano Lutes

During the Renaissance, several sizes of instruments were produced to make up families corresponding more or less to the different registers of the human voice. Small lutes replicated the soprano register.

These two lutes, with their knotted-gut frets, are based on an instrument by Wendelin Tieffenbrucker which is preserved in the Kunsthistorisches Museum in Vienna. Tieffenbrucker belonged to a German family famous for its lute making in the sixteenth and seventeenth centuries. Half of the family settled in northern Italy and the other half in Lyon, France. Wendelin was very active in Padua toward the mid-sixteenth century.

Like all of Edward Turner's instruments, these lutes are meticulously crafted and historically faithful to the originals. A Gothic-style rose ornaments the soundboard.

OPUS 56

Renaissance Soprano Lute
In the manner of Wendelin Tieffenbrucker
By Edward R. Turner
Vancouver, British Columbia
1974
Spruce, British Columbia yew and maple, ebony, Quebec maple, gut, pearwood, ivory, nylon
Overall length: 33.2 cm;
body: 20.5 x 12.6 cm; depth: 6.5 cm;
peg box: 10 cm
CCFCS 74-695

Above: *Close-up view of the Gothic-style rose.*

OPUS 55

Renaissance Soprano Lute
In the manner of Wendelin Tieffenbrucker
By Edward R. Turner
Vancouver, British Columbia
1974
Spruce, British Columbia yellow cedar, basswood, ebony, maple, boxwood, gut, pearwood, ivory, nylon
Overall length: 33.8 cm;
body: 21.5 x 12.6 cm; depth: 6.3 cm;
peg box: 10 cm
CCFCS 74-694

Opus 57 – Baroque Lute

While the lute declined in popularity in France, it continued to develop in Germany in the late seventeenth century. The eleven-course lute, which was used in France and Germany, acquired two more courses, strung on an extension of the peg box on the same side as the low-pitched strings. This innovation made it possible to play low notes and thus gave the lute a broader musical repertoire. The works of Sylvius Leopold Weiss, one of the leading lutenists and composers for the thirteen-course lute, contributed significantly to the development of this music.

Rose inspired by Islamic art.

Richard Berg fashioned this lute after a Renaissance instrument built by Hans Burkholzer in 1596, which was converted into a baroque lute by Tomas Edlinger in 1705. The original ivory instrument is preserved in the Kunsthistorisches Museum in Vienna. The body is constructed of Brazilian rosewood; the German spruce soundboard is embellished with a rose designed by Berg; and the neck is made of ebony plywood. The courses, the first two of which consist of single strings, are tuned to A=415 and thus reproduce the D-minor chord and scale. Berg concentrates a great deal on the visual aesthetics of his instruments, whose physical features, he says, should reflect the quality of the sound.

Richard Berg

While luthier Richard Berg strives for impeccable tone, he is fascinated by the aesthetics of instrument making. In fact, it was the variety of the lute's shapes and decorations that first attracted him to lute making. Before that, his love of the flamenco guitar led him to Spain, where he visited numerous guitar makers' workshops. In 1973, he built his first guitar, "just to see if [he] could do it." Berg continued his research independently and constructed his first lute in 1975. Drawing on the resources of the American Lute Society, he received valuable advice from experienced luthiers and found a major source

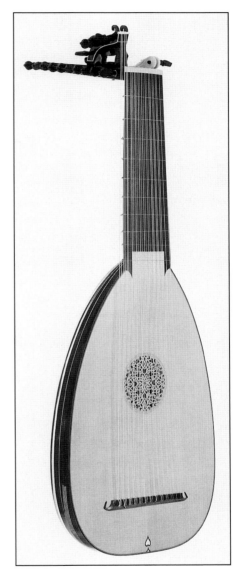

OPUS 57

Baroque Lute
In the manner of Hans Burkholzer and Tomas Edlinger
By Richard Berg
Ottawa, Ontario
1992
Brazilian rosewood, German spruce, ebony, plum, recycled ivory, plastic, gut
Body: 50.5 x 33.2 cm; depth: 17.5 cm
CCFCS 92-155

of inspiration in his discussions with musicians. He was particularly influenced by Toyohiko Sato, an internationally renowned baroque lutenist, who now owns several of Berg's instruments.

In 1983, Berg received a Canada Council grant to visit European luthiers and musicians, and study, photograph and draw instruments in museum collections. He has crafted Renaissance and baroque lutes, theorbos, chitarrones, archlutes, and classical guitars. While Berg uses original historic instruments as inspiration and strives to preserve their spirit, he does not attempt to build replicas, preferring instead to tailor the instruments to the needs and tastes of his clients. Although not a full-time luthier, Richard Berg has a distinguished reputation and a clientèle of North American, European and Asian musicians.

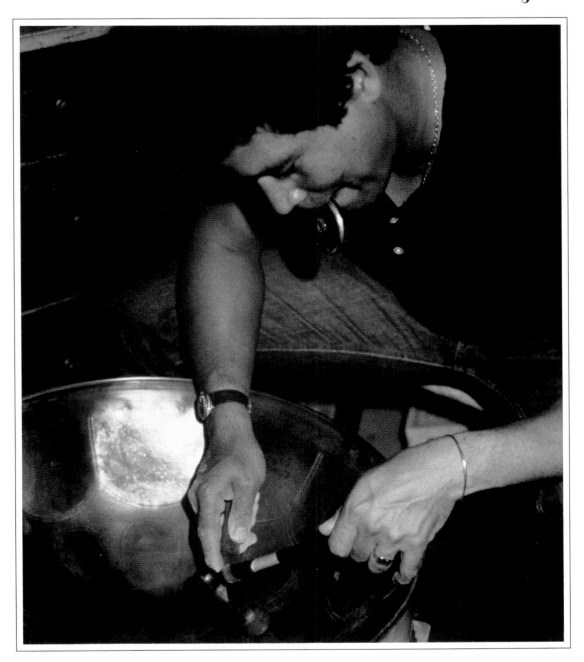

French-style ornament painted by Danièle Forget on a Beaupré harpsichord. The bird symbolizes the new life given to the tree that was felled to make the instrument.

Folk traditions (myths, legends and songs) and visual arts are sources of information on the symbolic values connected with musical instruments, as represented by their shape, their ornamentation, and even the material used to make them. Through these symbolic media, human beings communicate their vision of the world and their understanding of the universe.

As noted earlier, Renaissance and baroque luthiers were familiar with the concept of the "golden mean," a mathematical formula based on the proportions of the human body (see chapter on "Aesthetics"). But the similarities between musical instruments and the human shape extend far beyond this abstract formula. The contours of stringed instruments evoke body shapes, as is vividly illustrated in photographer Man Ray's work *Violon d'Ingres*, in which two *f*s like those

on the soundboard of a violin are superimposed on a woman's naked back.

Interestingly enough, instruments are usually displayed or photographed not in their playing position, but in an upright position like that of a person standing. Some parts of musical instruments are even named after parts of the body, for example, the waist, ribs and neck. Contrary to the conventional wisdom, the instrument is not an extension but a representation of the body.

Renaissance luthiers conveyed the notion of harmony between humans and the universe through the motif of two triangles, one inverted and superimposed on the other. This motif forms the basis of numerous rose designs on lutes and other stringed instruments of that era. The roses, often highly elaborate, are sculpted in two main styles, Gothic and Arab. The first is purely decorative and imitates the roses of Gothic cathedrals, while the second encompasses a wealth of symbolic elements.

Previous page: *Earle Wong, tuning a steel drum in Toronto, 1991.*

The use of musical instruments in religious ceremonies, in celebrations, and at important events — not to mention their use by various cultural communities — is indicative of the social significance of the musical instrument. In the Middle Ages, the psaltery, the organ and the harp were associated with religious music. Gregory the Great described the psaltery as soft, delicate, and pointing to the sky. The drum and other percussion instruments along with the rebec (medieval violin) and the horn were in the realm of secular music; Satan is sometimes depicted playing the drum, surrounded by the other instruments. The cymbals, made of bronze (an alloy of copper and tin), and the cornett were symbols of hell and were thus prohibited by the Church.

Traditional musical instruments are often symbols of ethnicity. The Celtic harp is the emblem of Ireland; the panpipe is associated with Romania, the bouzouki with Greece, the steel drums with Trinidad, and so on. These instruments play an important social role in that their shape and the music played on them express a sense of belonging to a culture and a tradition.

This chapter illustrates some facets of symbolism: symbolism of materials, symbolism of sounds, and symbolic instruments. The reader may also wish to refer to the instruments in preceding chapters to explore the secrets in their colours, shapes and decorative motifs.

Symbolism of Materials
Ceramic Instruments

Opus 58 and 59 – Flutes

Flutes can be made from a wide variety of materials. For a long time, the preferred material in Europe was wood, but ivory, porcelain and even glass flutes appeared, especially during the baroque period. The modern flute tends to be made of silver, gold, platinum or plastic. Bamboo plays an important role in Oriental cultures. In addition to wooden flutes, bone, ceramic and copper flutes are found in various parts of the world.

Earth is a symbol of fertility, wealth and generosity. In many cultures, ceramic instruments express the desire to unite earth and music in order to supplicate the benevolent spirits and elicit their favour.

The ceramic flutes and drums presented here are often associated with various musical traditions. The breath that produces sound in the wind instrument is a symbol of life, while the beating of the drum symbolizes the human heart. The union of these two instruments has given rise to a French proverb: "What comes from the flute goes back to the drum."

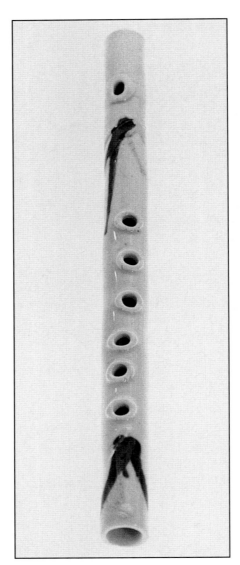

OPUS 58

Flute
By Tony Bloom
Canmore, Alberta
Circa 1985
Porcelain
32.5 cm
CCFCS 85-226.1-3
Inscribed with the artist's signature and seal.
Gift of the Massey Foundation

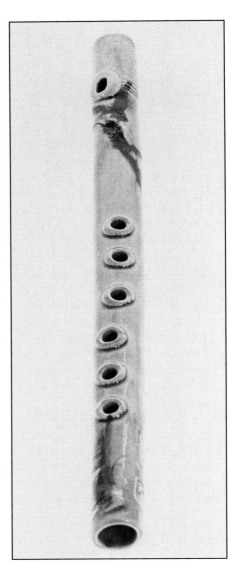

OPUS 59

Flute
By Tony Bloom
Canmore, Alberta
1977
Stoneware
37.8 cm
CCFCS 83-361.1-4
Inscribed with the artist's signature and seal.
Gift of the Massey Foundation

Tony Bloom

Instrument making comes naturally to ceramist and musician Tony Bloom. Spurred by a desire to build a flute for his musician brother, he began experimenting with pottery and instrument making in Canmore. A few months after taking courses at the Banff School of Fine Arts, he became a professional artist and potter. Also a drummer, he has fashioned several darabukkas (small Arabian drums). Tony Bloom has produced bas-reliefs and sculptures in addition to musical instruments.

Opus 60 – Darabukka

Along with a few other percussion instruments such as claves (or rhythm sticks), the drum is one of the earliest musical instruments. The concept of attaching a hide to a receptacle, such as a pot or tree trunk, appears to have originated in the neolithic era. The drum is often associated with dance; but, because of its strong primal rhythm, it has also been vested with magical powers and used in sacred and religious rites by several cultures.

According to Tony Bloom, this instrument is a hybrid—a blend of the Arab darabukka and the Indian tabla. The stoneware pot is covered with an iron-oxide glaze.

OPUS 60

Darabukka
By Tony Bloom
Canmore, Alberta
Circa 1985
Stoneware, goatskin
Diameter: 25.5 cm; height: 22.3 cm
CCFCS 85-561
Inscribed with the artist's
signature and seal.
Gift of the Massey Foundation

Opus 61 – Flute

This porcelain flute is covered with a brown glaze.

Martin Breton

A ceramist for fifteen years, Martin Breton trained extensively in Quebec and France. He has been making ceramic musical instruments since 1983. After a trip to Morocco, where he discovered the world of percussion instruments, he began making darabukkas. Around the same time, an order from a group of African musicians touring Quebec introduced Breton to udu making. Martin Breton has also crafted wind instruments, such as the ocarina, which he makes in the shape of birds and animals, and the flute.

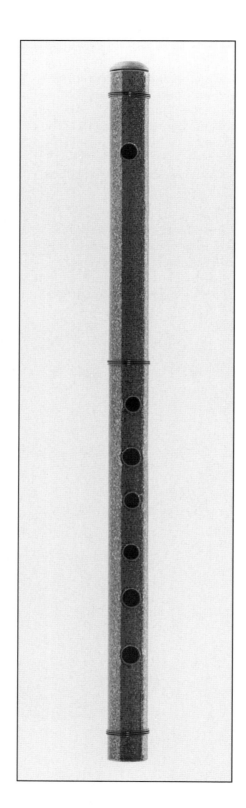

OPUS 61

Flute
By Martin Breton
Sainte-Agathe-de-Lotbinière, Quebec
1984
Porcelain
44.5 cm
CCFCS 84-143

Opus 62 – Ocarina

The European version of the ocarina appears to have been invented in Italy around 1860, but this type of flute has existed for a very long time in South America, Asia and Africa. This instrument by Martin Breton is a variant of the globular flute.

Breton's bird-shaped instruments are in keeping with ancient traditions like that of the Aztecs, who fashioned their globular flutes in animal or human shapes. The Italian term *ocarina* means "little goose."

OPUS 62

Ocarina
By Martin Breton
Sainte-Agathe-de-Lotbinière, Quebec
1984
Porcelain
Diameter: 6.9 cm; height: 10.2 cm
CCFCS 84-134

Opus 63 to 68 – Darabukkas

All of Martin Breton's drums are made of untreated stoneware and fired in a wood-burning kiln. Pieces of *babiche* (thin leather strips, thongs or laces) are used to attach the drumhead to the body.

OPUS 64

Darabukka
By Martin Breton
Sainte-Agathe-de-Lotbinière, Quebec
1984
Stoneware, cowhide, babiche
Diameter: 27.4 cm; height: 34.5 cm
CCFCS 84-138

OPUS 63

Darabukka
By Martin Breton
Sainte-Agathe-de-Lotbinière,
Quebec
1984
Stoneware, cowhide, babiche
Diameter: 29.3 cm;
height: 36.6 cm
CCFCS 84-137

OPUS 65

Darabukka
By Martin Breton
Sainte-Agathe-de-Lotbinière,
Quebec
1984
Stoneware, cowhide, babiche
Diameter: 20.9 cm; height: 32 cm
CCFCS 84-139

OPUS 66

Darabukka
By Martin Breton
Sainte-Agathe-de-Lotbinière, Quebec
1984
Stoneware, cowhide, babiche
Diameter: 25 cm; height: 30.5 cm
CCFCS 84-140

OPUS 67

Darabukka
By Martin Breton
Sainte-Agathe-de-Lotbinière, Quebec
1984
Stoneware, cowhide, babiche
Diameter: 17 cm; height: 27.2 cm
CCFCS 84-141

OPUS 68

Darabukka
By Martin Breton
Sainte-Agathe-de-Lotbinière, Quebec
1984
Stoneware, cowhide, babiche
Diameter: 15 cm; height: 17.2 cm
CCFCS 84-142

Opus 69 and 70 – Udus

The udu consists of a ceramic pot with a hole in the side. The musician alternately covers the top and side openings with the palms of the hands, producing sound through the compression and release of air inside the pot. The udu is thus an aerophone, as air is the element that vibrates and resonates. This type of instrument is found in Nigeria, mostly among the Ibos.

When Martin Breton received an order for an udu in 1983, he built it according to an instrument that had been brought to Quebec by an African troupe of performers.

OPUS 69

Udu
By Martin Breton
Sainte-Agathe-de-Lotbinière, Quebec
1984
Stoneware
Diameter: 27 cm; height: 30.8 cm
CCFCS 84-135

OPUS 70

Udu
By Martin Breton
Sainte-Agathe-de-Lotbinière, Quebec
1984
Stoneware
Diameter: 19.5 cm; height: 24.5 cm
CCFCS 84-156

Symbolism of Sounds

Opus 71 and 72 – Bells

*I*ts powerful, penetrating sound made the bell a major means of communication in many societies. It marked the hours of the day, signalled important events, summoned people together, invoked the spirits, and punctuated rituals. It also sounded warnings, repelled lightning, heralded births, and paid a final tribute to the dead. The hand bells with clappers already in use in ancient times were made of bronze or pottery.

Christina Kloepfer casts her bells in bronze. Opus 71 is similar in shape to African double bells (which, however, are struck from the outside). Opus 72 has a more traditional shape.

Christina Kloepfer

Christina Kloepfer graduated from the Sheridan College School of Design in 1973. After apprenticing under sculptor Jordi Bonet in Montréal and Frank Colson in Florida, she opened her own studio in 1978. Fascinated with bronze, particularly its durability, she uses the

OPUS 71

Bell
By Christina Kloepfer
Kitchener, Ontario
Circa 1983
Bronze
Overall width and height: 11 x 8.6 cm;
diameter of each bell: 5 cm
CCFCS 83-235
Gift of the Massey Foundation

lost-wax method of casting. Through her work with metal, Kloepfer says she is carrying on a family tradition, as her grandfather was a blacksmith.

For this artist, bell making combines two important elements: formal research, which allows for artistic expression, and technical research (on the choice of diameter, thickness, alloy and so on), which is reflected in utilitarian, functional objects. The result is beauty of shape complemented by beauty of sound. Christina Kloepfer's bells have been displayed in a number of exhibitions across Canada.

OPUS 72
Bell
By Christina Kloepfer
Kitchener, Ontario
Circa 1983
Bronze
Diameter: 7.2 cm; height: 7.5 cm
CCFCS 83-236
Gift of the Massey Foundation

Opus 73 – Violin

The violin is associated with harmonious, appealing and seductive sounds that can charm or captivate the listener, as numerous tales and legends from French Canada and elsewhere reveal. Characters in "Les marionnettes," "Le violon magique" and "La légende de Rose Latulippe" grapple with the almost magical powers attributed to the violin. Used for entertainment, the violin had a dubious reputation and was regarded suspiciously by the Church.

Michael Baran based this violin on a model by Antonio Stradivari and named it "Dorothea."

Michael Baran

A native of Czechoslovakia, Michael Baran immigrated to Canada in 1928. His interest in violin making began when he was around nine years old. After acquiring experience by repairing numerous violins, he made his first instrument in 1937. Baran also taught himself to play the violin as a teenager, inspired by the performances of gypsies at popular celebrations in his native land. Having a trade in addition to his work as a luthier always enabled Michael Baran to generously give his violins to young musicians who could not afford to buy them.

Opus 74 – Violin

This modified Stradivarius has a soundboard in three parts.

Fernand Schryer

Fernand Schryer learned violin making from his grandfather. Making his living as a fisherman, he could not find the time to engage in instrument making until he was in his 40s. But, since his retirement, he has devoted himself full time to the art. To date, he has made 300 violins. Schryer prefers to use local wood, which he cuts himself and which he dries for years before using.

Opus 75 – Aeolian Harp

The harp of Aeolus, which is said to make the wind sing, has roots in a number of legends: the invention of the lyre is attributed to the god Hermes, who let the wind blow over dried sinews in a tortoiseshell; and David's harp was purportedly made to sing by the breath of God. Even today, the Aeolian harp retains a slightly magical aura, as only hypothetical explanations have been found to account for the sounds produced by the wind's movement through its strings.

Around 1650, the German theoretician Kircher devised the Aeolian harp, using the ancient

OPUS 73

Violin
By Michael Baran
Toronto, Ontario
1973
Eastern sycamore, giant redwood
Overall length: 59 cm;
body: 35.7 x 20.2 cm; ribs: 3 cm
CCFCS 73-1063
Gift of Michael Baran

OPUS 74

Violin
By Fernand Schryer
Pointe-au-Chêne, Quebec
1980
Maple, spruce
Overall length: 60.4 cm;
body: 36 x 21 cm; ribs: 3.1 cm
CCFCS 81-333

principle of wind blowing over stretched strings. But it was not until a century later that the harp become popular, particularly in England. An instrument conveying the voice of nature was certain to inspire poets and writers at a time when burgeoning romanticism glorified nature. The Aeolian harp was thus the source of several poems.

This harp continued to be popular until the mid-nineteenth century. In England, it was set on windowsills in the home. On the continent, it was found in gardens, grottoes, summer homes and even vacant castles. Perhaps certain "ghosts" were nothing more than puffs of wind whirling between the strings of a strategically placed Aeolian harp.

David Johnson

A carpenter in his spare time, David Johnson enjoys working with and sculpting wood. As he has always liked music, he combines his interests by making instruments: several variants of the dulcimer, Celtic harp and Aeolian harp. He began making this unusual instrument after a friend, who had read about the Aeolian harp, sketched one for him. Intrigued, Johnson was tempted to experiment and eventually adapted the instrument so that it could be placed in a vertical position outside the house.

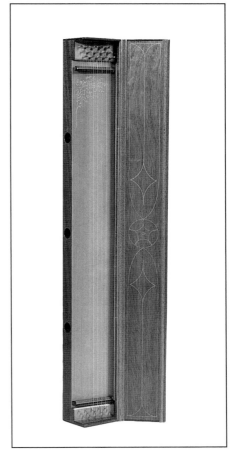

OPUS 75

Aeolian Harp
By David Johnson
Rimbey, Alberta
Circa 1982
Spruce, mahogany, nylon, metal, rosewood
106 x 21 x 19 cm
Lent by David Johnson

Symbolic Instruments
Folk Instruments of North American Origin

Opus 76 and 77 – Banjos

The banjo is a modern adaptation of an instrument played by west African slaves in the New World beginning in the seventeenth century. In Martinique, among other countries, it was associated with the *calinda* dance, which was later banned by the settlers. The banjo was popularized by black minstrels in the United States in the early twentieth century and subsequently marketed in its present form in the United States and England.

The two banjos shown here are identical. The frame is made of maple plywood, and the neck of maple and walnut plywood, decorated on the back with a double purfling. The peg box is shaped like a stylized violin.

Thomas Dorward

Thomas Dorward was born and grew up in Denver, Colorado. He built his first instrument, a classical guitar, when he was still in high school and had already made three guitars by the time he entered the University of Michigan to study psychology. During his three years of studies, he repaired and constructed musical instruments. In 1969, he enrolled at Dalhousie University to develop his skill and made

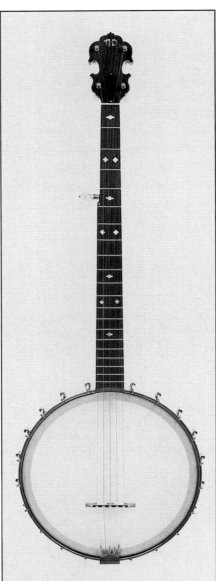
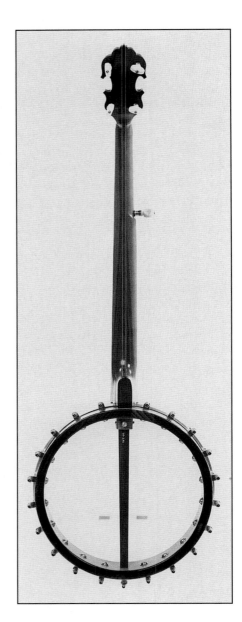

OPUS 76 and 77

Banjos
By Thomas Dorward
Halifax, Nova Scotia
1974
Maple, walnut, rosewood, abalone, mother-of-pearl, plastic, metal
Overall length: 90 cm; diameter of body: 29 cm; sides: 7 cm
CCFCS 74-240 and 74-241

several types of instruments, including guitars, Appalachian dulcimers and banjos. Shortly after his graduation, he and his wife, Marla, opened the Halifax Folklore Centre to buy, sell, trade, repair and construct stringed instruments; they later broadened their scope to include a large amount of repair work on instruments of the violin family. For fifteen years or so, Thomas Dorward has been particularly interested in making archtop instruments; he has also added the American A-Style Mandolin to his line of instruments.

Opus 78 and 79
Appalachian Dulcimers

These identical dulcimers have a beautiful hourglass-shaped soundbox similar to that of instruments from north-western Europe, particularly the *épinette des Vosges*. It is derived from the zithers that European immigrants brought to the United States in the eighteenth century. While the instrument is found throughout the United States and Canada, little is known about its North American origins. The Appalachian dulcimer is used to accompany singing and in combination with the concertina and hurdy-gurdy to accompany dancing.

Traditional heart-shaped motifs embellish the soundboard of these walnut dulcimers with rosewood peg boxes, and a simple scroll graces the head. Each instrument has three strings.

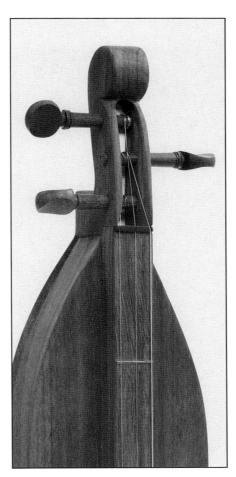

OPUS 78 and 79

Appalachian Dulcimers
By Thomas Dorward
Halifax, Nova Scotia
1974
Walnut, rosewood
Overall length by width: 92 x 15.2 cm;
sides: 6 cm
CCFCS 74-244 and 74-245

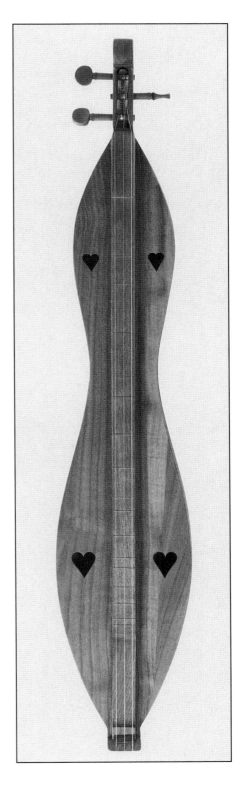

Opus 80 and 81 – Banjos

Based on the traditional banjo, each of these identical instruments consists of a circular wooden soundboard with a membrane stretched over a metal ring in the middle. The neck has no frets, and the head is outfitted with four pegs. A fifth peg is located on the side of the neck to attach a fifth string, which is shorter than the others and is used to play the melody.

OPUS 80 and 81

Banjos
By Oskar Graf
Clarendon, Ontario
1974
Black cherry, ebony, metal, plastic
Overall length: 91 cm; diameter of body: 25 cm; sides: 5 cm
CCFCS 74-236 and 74-237
Ink marking: "Made by Oskar Graf 3/74 Clarendon, Ont."

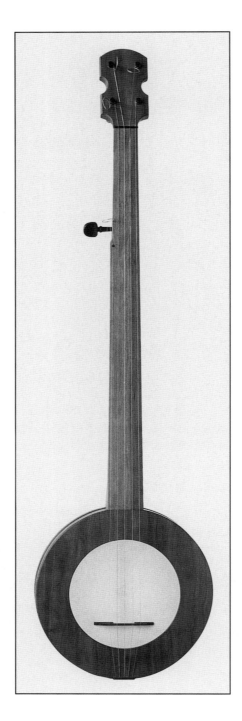
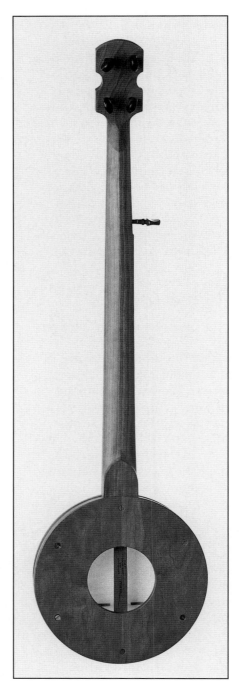

Opus 82 and 83
Mandolin-Banjos

Nineteenth-century instrument makers experimented in creating hybrid instruments, such as the mandolin-banjo, for which August Polmann patented his drawing in 1885. The instruments shown here, which follow Polmann's drawing, have the long neck, five strings (including the melody string) and flat back of the banjo.

The soundboard, with its soundhole, is derived from the mandolin, while the shape of the body is a compromise between the perfectly circular shape of the banjo and the half-pear shape of the classical mandolin. These instruments, both meticulously crafted, may be related to the flat-backed model known as the American mandolin, which appeared at the turn of the century in the United States.

OPUS 82 and 83

Mandolin-Banjos
In the manner of August Polmann
By Oskar Graf
Clarendon, Ontario
1974
Honduran mahogany, spruce, holly, ebony, mother-of-pearl, metal, plastic
Overall length: 86 cm; diameter of body: 26 cm; sides: 7 cm
CCFCS 74-238 and 74-259

Opus 84 and 85
Appalachian Dulcimers

The soundboard of these hourglass-shaped instruments is made of cedar and decorated with four trillium-shaped openings, and the sides and back are in black cherry. There are four strings and a fingerboard with seventeen metal frets.

OPUS 84 and 85

Appalachian Dulcimers
By Oskar Graf
Clarendon, Ontario
1973
Black cherry, British Columbia cedar, ebony, bubinga wood, metal
Overall length: 92 cm; diameter of body: 16.5 cm; sides: 7 cm
CCFCS 74-242 and 74-243

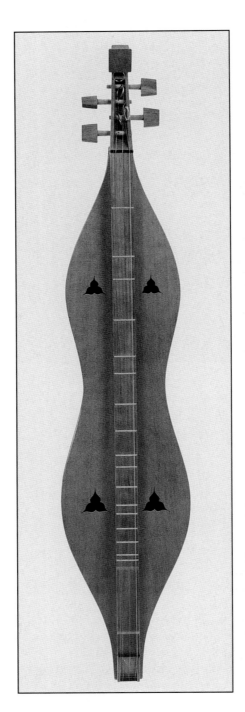

Opus 86
Appalachian Dulcimer

A scroll graces the head
of this sleek instrument. The
soundboard has four clover-
shaped soundholes.

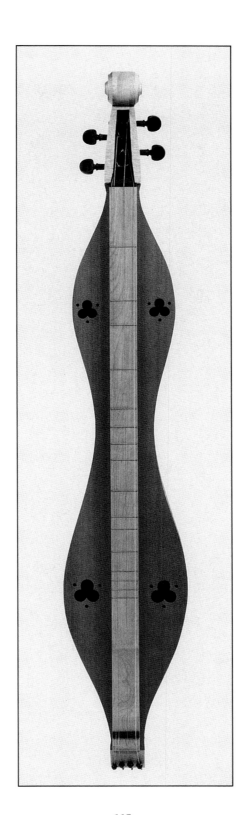

OPUS 86

Appalachian Dulcimer
By David Miller
Saskatoon, Saskatchewan
1979
Cedar, ebony, maple, agate
Overall length: 94 cm; diameter of
body: 16 cm; sides: 7.3 cm
CCFCS 85-668
Gift of the Massey Foundation

Opus 87
Appalachian Dulcimer

To play this unusually shaped instrument, the right hand plucks the strings with a plectrum while the left hand plays the melody by pressing a small stick against the frets located under the first string.

While the playing technique and number of strings for this instrument are those of the traditional dulcimer, the fingerboard is shorter, ending at the rose. The bridge, which is centred on the broadest part of the soundboard, is outfitted with a brass tailpiece. In contrast, the traditional Appalachian dulcimer is equipped with a central fingerboard running the entire length of the body; a nut and saddle at either end support the strings.

Rickey Lair

Rickey Lair made his first guitar after completing a community college programme in design. His primary concern is with the quality and beauty of the woodwork. The trademark of Lair's instruments, which include guitars and dulcimers, is their highly personal design. The elegant, refined lines are evidence of painstaking craftsmanship.

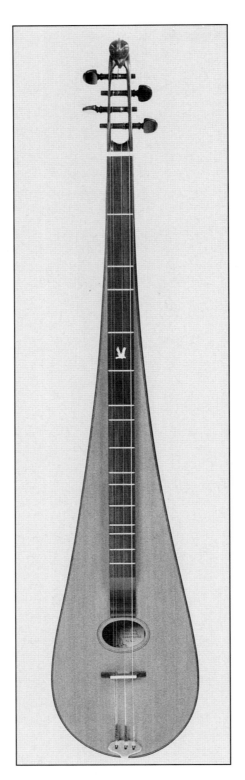

OPUS 87

Appalachian Dulcimer
By Rickey Lair
Dorchester, New Brunswick
Circa 1980
Rosewood, mahogany, spruce, mother-of-pearl
Overall length: 90 cm; diameter of body: 17 cm; sides: 7.4 cm
CCFCS 83-749.1-3
Gift of the Massey Foundation

Above: *The carved bird's head that graces this dulcimer adds to the instrument's elegance.*

Left: *Notice the bird in flight inlaid on the fingerboard.*

Opus 88 – Banjo

This superb banjo is inlaid with mother-of-pearl on the neck and has a gold-plated metal resonator, which produces a striking visual effect. It has only four strings; the melody string, usually attached to a peg on the side of the neck, is absent.

George Kindness

Born in 1888, George Kindness learned the luthier's craft in his native Edinburgh. After settling in Canada in 1911, he worked for the large Toronto workshop of R.S. William & Sons, where he made numerous violins. He owned his own workshop in Toronto from 1921 to 1931 and then worked as a cabinetmaker for the Robert Simpson Company for fifteen years, while continuing to make violins and other stringed instruments. In 1946, with the help of his son Robert, he again opened his own workshop. George Kindness built approximately 150 violins, many of which are played by professional musicians.

OPUS 88

Banjo
By George Kindness
Toronto, Ontario
1933
Wood, gold-plated metal, mother-of-pearl
Overall length: 85 cm; diameter of body: 34.5 cm; sides: 62 cm
CCFCS 85-62
Gift of Phyllis Kindness

Opus 89 and 90 – Dulcimers

his gentle-sounding instrument is also called the *dulce melos*, from which the name "dulcimer" was derived. Probably of Persian origin, the dulcimer appeared in Italian paintings in the mid-fifteenth century.

The dulcimer is a preeminent traditional instrument. In the British Isles, it accompanies reels, jigs and hornpipes. In Hungary, a similar but larger instrument, the *cimbalom*, accompanies traditional dances. The dulcimer also plays a role in symphonic works.

OPUS 89

Dulcimer
By Bob Rowland
Scarborough, Ontario
1973
Walnut, birch, maple, poplar, oak, steel
Length by width: 106 x 59 cm; sides: 11.5 cm
CCFCS 74-234

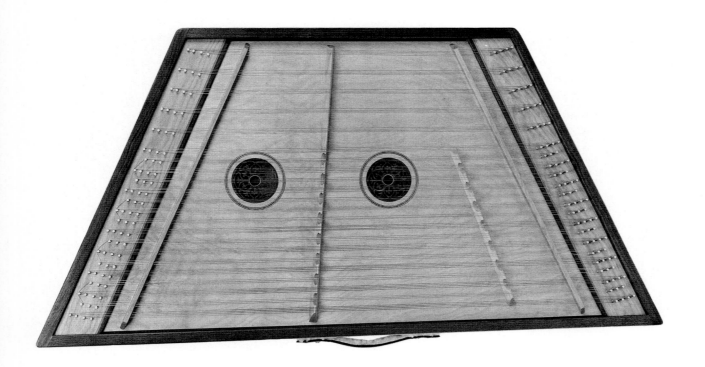

OPUS 90

Dulcimer
By Bob Rowland
Scarborough, Ontario
1973
Walnut, birch, maple, poplar, oak, steel
Length by width: 106 x 59 cm;
sides: 11.5 cm
CCFCS 74-235

This close-up view of the soundboard clearly reveals the grain of the birch wood.

Opus 91 – Celtic Harp

One of the world's most ancient instruments, the harp appeared in Europe around the ninth century. It is considered a noble instrument, associated with King David, who is often portrayed holding one in paintings. In Ireland and Scotland, the harp, known in Gaelic as *clàrsach*, enjoyed a prominent position beginning in the tenth century. It was used until the eighteenth century and became Ireland's emblem.

In the early nineteenth century, during the burgeoning Celtic revival in Dublin and Edinburgh, organizations such as the Dublin Harp Society were established to restore the tradition of the harp. John Egan, a Dublin instrument maker, invented a modern clàrsach for novice musicians. Lighter in construction, this harp had gut strings and hand-operated levers to raise the pitch of the strings by a semitone. The instrument is sometimes called the Celtic or neo-Irish harp.

Based on the modern clàrsach, the harp shown here has thirty strings, made of nylon. The soundbox, which consists of a single piece of carved cedar

OPUS 91

Celtic Harp
By Tim Hobrough
Vancouver, British Columbia
1974
Maple, cedar, nylon, steel, brass
Height: 99 cm; base: 29 x 20 cm
CCFCS 74-591.1-2

taken from a church organ pipe, bears a traditional "magical knot" motif, and the head of the pillar is decorated with a stylized bird.

Tim Hobrough

Tim Hobrough has been making instruments since 1972. After apprenticing for two years under Michael Dunn in Vancouver, he received a Canada Council grant in 1976 to study early harps in European collections. He settled in Scotland in 1978 and opened a workshop in the village of Beauly in 1989. He crafts a wide array of harps, including medieval, Renaissance, baroque, Irish and Celtic, and medieval instruments such as the dulcimer, psaltery and lyre.

Opus 92 – Bouzouki

The bouzouki is the instrument par excellence of traditional Greek music. In the early twentieth century, it was associated with the underworld and was consequently banned by the authorities; some musicians were even persecuted. In the 1930s, however, it regained public favour through sound recordings and film scores, which made it known the world over.

The bouzouki that is played today has usually been adapted for Western music. The traditional instrument underwent changes similar to those made to the guitar and the mandolin, acquiring metal frets, machine heads, and four courses of strings. In fact, the bouzouki is a long-necked lute played with a plectrum. The body, with its rounded back, is lined inside with a thin metal sheet that gives the instrument its characteristic timbre. The strings are the same length as those of a guitar.

The body of the instrument shown here is made of walnut and strips of ash, and the soundboard is made of spruce. It is decorated with black plastic and imitation mother-of-pearl.

Constantin Tingas

Constantin Tingas was born of Greek parents in Trois-Rivières, Quebec. At a very early age, he moved to Greece, where he lived until the age of fifteen. After learning the basics of the luthier's craft from his grandfather, Tingas studied for a year and a half at the international school of stringed-instrument making in Verona, Italy. He worked for several months in the

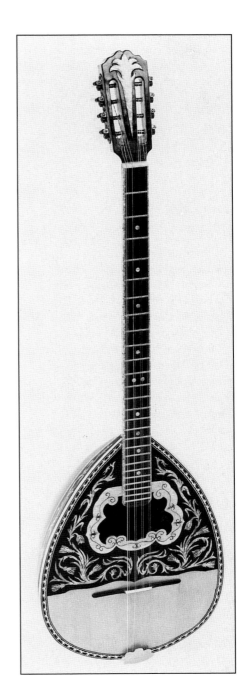

OPUS 92

Bouzouki
By Constantin Tingas
Toronto, Ontario
1991
Walnut, ash, spruce, linden, ebony,
African padouk, plastic
Overall length: 98.5 cm;
body: 38.5 x 30 cm; depth: 18.5 cm
CCFCS 91-456.1-2

workshops of the famous Parisian guitar maker Robert Bouchet. Upon his return to Canada at the age of twenty-three, he abandoned instrument making in order to study aeronautical engineering in Toronto. In 1971, Constantin Tingas resumed instrument making and opened a workshop, where he has built many violins, violas, violoncellos, guitars and traditional Greek instruments, such as the bouzouki, the *baglama*, the *tzouras* and the *laouto* (or Greek lute).

Opus 93 and 94
Baglama and Tzouras

The baglama and the tzouras are small, long-necked lutes derived from the bouzouki. The three instruments make up the typical ensemble associated with *rebetiko* music and songs. This music, with its strong Turkish influence, appeared in Greek port cities late in the last century. It soon became the music of the streets and cafés, associated with a tough milieu. In the 1920s, the baglama and

OPUS 93

Baglama
By Constantin Tingas
Toronto, Ontario
1991
Maple, ebony, spruce, linden,
African padouk
Overall length: 57 cm;
body: 16 x 12 cm; depth: 6 cm
CCFCS 91-454

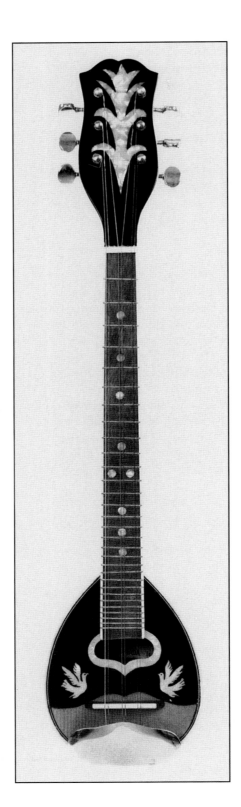

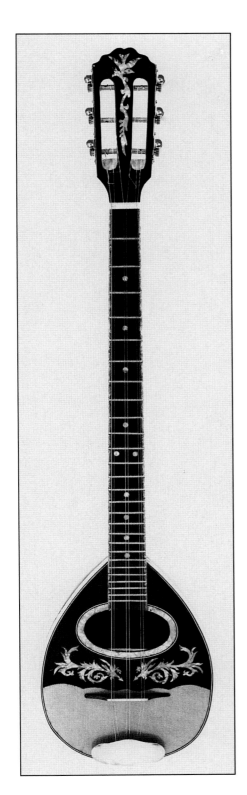

the tzouras met with the same social disfavour as the bouzouki. Today, the popularity of these instruments has been restored by virtuoso Greek musicians.

OPUS 94

Tzouras
By Constantin Tingas
Toronto, Ontario
1991
Walnut, ash, spruce, linden, ebony,
African padouk, plastic
Overall length: 87.5 cm;
body: 27.5 x 20.5 cm; depth: 15 cm
CCFCS 91-457.1-2

Opus 95 – Lyra

Originating in the Greek islands, the lyra is used mostly on Crete and in the Dodecanese. Traditionally, only men played it, to perform dance music. Until the middle of this century, small bells were attached to the bow to provide rhythmic accompaniment. Today, when it is not replaced by the violin, the lyra may be played alone or with instruments such as the laouto, the *daouli* drum, and *dachares* tambourines. It is also played with Western instruments.

The body of this lyra was carved from a single piece of mahogany. The soundboard is made of spruce.

OPUS 95

Lyra
By Constantin Tingas
Toronto, Ontario
1991
Honduran mahogany, spruce
Overall length: 55 cm;
body: 28 x 21 cm;
depth: 5 cm
CCFCS 91-455

Opus 96 and 97 – Panpipes

Popular in traditional Romanian music, the panpipe is used by *lautaris*, or professional musicians, to play dance pieces and other selections. The instruments shown here were made in Canada by Valeriu Apan, known for his interpretation of popular Romanian and Western music.

Valeriu Apan

Romanian musician Valeriu Apan settled in the Edmonton area after coming to Canada in 1980 to give a series of concerts. He subsequently became the director and arranger of the Romanian Choral Group of Edmonton. Apan was introduced to the folk music of his native country at the age of twelve by an uncle who taught him to play the traditional music of Romanian shepherds. He entered the Cluj conservatory, where he studied musicology and composition, and learned to play the piano and violin. He developed a keen interest in the panpipe at this time. But, as the only such instruments on the market were mass-produced and of poor quality, Valeriu Apan began to make his own panpipes, producing fifty of them by 1984.

OPUS 96

Panpipe
By Valeriu Apan
Edmonton, Alberta
1982
Plum, bamboo, beeswax
Overall length: 36.5 cm;
pipe lengths: 6.5 to 25.5 cm
CCFCS 85-46

OPUS 97

Panpipe
By Valeriu Apan
Edmonton, Alberta
1983
Bamboo
Overall length: 43 cm;
pipe lengths: 7.5 to 33.5 cm
CCFCS 86-119

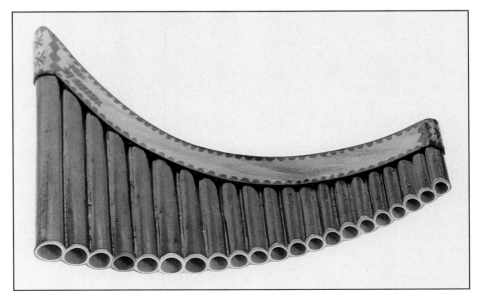

Opus 98 – Tilinca

The tilinca is one of the many traditional Romanian flutes. It is hard to imagine a simpler instrument: it consists of a copper tube which is open at both ends and which has no finger holes. Melodies are produced by altering the force of the breath while alternately opening and closing the embouchure. The tilinca accompanies songs and dances and is also played as a solo instrument.

OPUS 98

Tilinca
By Valeriu Apan
Edmonton, Alberta
1985
Wood, copper
55.6 cm
CCFCS 86-118

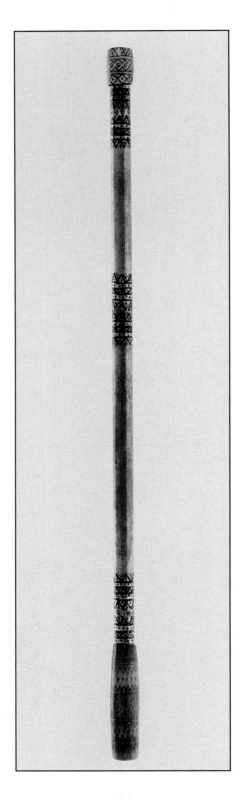

Opus 99 and 100 – Diatonic Accordions

The accordion originated in the nineteenth century, when it was developed by Cyrillus Demian, an Armenian instrument maker living in Vienna in 1829. Classified as an aerophone, it consists of a box containing free reeds, a keyboard made up of a row of buttons on the right, and a few keys on the left for producing chords. The central bellows cause air to make the free reeds resonate when the fingers release the flow of air by pressing a button. The diatonic accordion is equipped with a mechanism that makes it possible to produce a note when the bellows are compressed and another when they are expanded. This type of accordion has been made in the province of Quebec since the turn of the century, particularly by the Québec firm Gagné et Frères. Next to the violin, it is the most popular instrument for playing traditional dance music, especially in Quebec, but in other parts of Canada and the United States as well.

The meticulously crafted accordion shown here has four sets of reeds. It was made entirely by hand by Clément Breton, who lavished particular care on the marquetry.

Clément Breton

A native of Jonquière, Clément Breton has been making accordions for ten years. His passion for this instrument began when at the age of six he was enchanted by the concerts of his accordionist neighbour. Not until Breton was fifteen did he manage to obtain his

OPUS 99

Diatonic Accordion
By Clément Breton
Saint-Étienne-de-Lauzon, Quebec
1990–91
Makassar ebony, maple, kingwood, cardboard, chrome-plated iron, canvas, steel reeds, leather
Height: 28.5 cm; width (casings and closed bellows): 17 cm; depth: 16 cm
CCFCS 91-20.1-2

own accordion and enjoy playing the instrument. As he became increasingly interested in the different tones and chords produced by handmade accordions, he decided to explore accordion making. Although Clément Breton builds accordions in his spare time only, he has already produced twenty instruments, which are entirely handcrafted except for the Italian-made reeds.

Clément Breton, building an accordion in his workshop, 1991.

Gagné et Frères

Odilon Gagné (1852–1916) originally worked in wood and tinplate. Also an accordionist, he began repairing accordions and eventually turned to making them. In 1890 in Québec, he opened Gagné et Frères, a firm of artisans that made all parts of diatonic accordions on the premises. In addition, Odilon Gagné constructed approximately twenty pianos and several violins. His three sons, Wilfrid, Philias and Albert, also worked in the family business. Today, Gagné et Frères is a music store, but its owner, Paul-André Gagné, the founder's grandson, carries on the family's accordion-making tradition.

OPUS 100

Diatonic Accordion
By the firm of Gagné et Frères
Québec, Quebec
Circa 1910
Wood, metal, cardboard
Height: 26 cm; width (closed): 25 cm;
depth: 13 cm
CCFCS 84-144

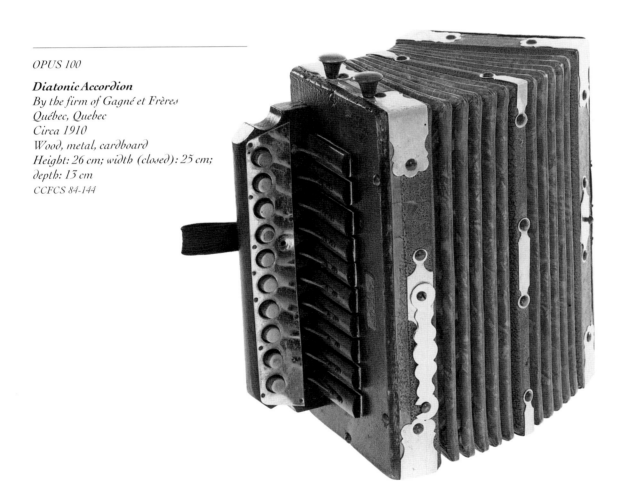

Opus 101 and 102 – Steel Drums

The instruments in a steel band are usually called *pans*. They are identified by the register in which they are tuned, for example, tenor pan and bass pan.

The steel drum is a recent invention, whose potential was discovered by Stree Simons in Trinidad in 1939. One end of an oil drum is hammered into a concave shape on which the position of the notes are grooved according to a set design and size. The diameter and depth of the note determine its pitch. The register (for example, tenor, alto or bass) is determined by the length of the drum-barrel, which is cut accordingly; an uncut barrel will produce a bass drum.

Earle Wong

A native of Trinidad, Earle Wong began playing steel drums at the age of twelve. After moving to Canada in 1968, he quickly earned recognition as a talented musician and organized Toronto's first steel band. Over the years, he has also become a master of the art of building and tuning steel drums—a traditional role for the head of a steel band, who usually makes and tunes his group's instruments. (Tuning a steel drum is the most complex, delicate step in making the

OPUS 101

Quadraphonic Steel Drums
By Earle Wong
Toronto, Ontario
1986
Chrome-plated steel
Diameter: 56.5 cm; height: 29 cm
CCFCS 86-226.1-7

instrument.) Earle Wong has participated in numerous workshops across Canada to share his expertise. He receives orders from across Canada and the United States, and has made drums for the Toronto Board of Education.

OPUS 102

Tenor Steel Drum
By Earle Wong
Toronto, Ontario
1986
Chrome-plated steel
Diameter: 56.5 cm; height: 19 cm
CCFCS 86-227

Conclusion

This far-from-exhaustive study of instrument making in Canada has been confined to artisans whose instruments are part of the Canadian Museum of Civilization's collection. There are many other talented instrument makers in Canada, some of whom loaned instruments to the Opus exhibition. These artisans are profiled below.

Nedd Kenney, wind-instrument maker

Wind-instrument maker Nedd Kenney is particularly interested in the Irish concert flute and the traditional Celtic flageolet. With over fifteen years' experience in performing Irish music, he came to instrument making through his search for a quality instrument. As the Irish concert flute is based on baroque flutes, he apprenticed under baroque-flute maker Jean-François Beaudin in 1989. Kenney established his own workshop in his native Prince Edward Island, where he works full-time and continues to perform. He is a founding member of the group Flying Tide, which specializes in Celtic and traditional Maritime music.

Jacques Martel, luthier

After training for three years under Italian master Sylvio de Lellis, Jacques Martel established his own workshop, L'atelier de lutherie, in Trois-Rivières in 1980. In addition to being especially interested in making instruments of the violin family, Martel restores stringed instruments. He has broadened his basic knowledge of the luthier's craft through extensive training with European masters. In particular, he studied varnish composition and the restoration and adjustment of string quartet instruments under Frédéric Boyer, and honed his knowledge of advanced restoration under Jean-Jacques Rampal.

Jacques Martel has received several grants from the ministère des Affaires culturelles du Québec and, in 1989, represented Quebec at the first Jeux de la francophonie in Morocco, where he won a gold medal for instrument making.

Iain Ro-Ha-Hes Phillips, luthier

Iain Phillips has been making musical instruments for close to twenty years. After discovering early music, he pursued studies in this field at the University of Ottawa. In response to the heavy demand for historic instruments, he spent much of the 1970s and 1980s making instruments, beginning with harps and eventually expanding his skill to other types of stringed instruments.

Phillips has several instruments to his credit, including viols, vitheles, *mandores*, *gigues* and medieval organs. He also teaches music history at Carleton University and heads an Ottawa baroque music group called Les barricades mystérieuses.

Thomas Strang, wind-instrument maker

Thomas Strang studied art restoration at Queen's University, and works as a scientific restorer at the Canadian Conservation Institute. In his free time, he makes wind instruments, an activity with many rewarding aspects: finding solutions to various technical challenges, perfecting a technique, researching quality raw materials and, finally, hearing the first sounds of the new instrument. One of the challenges that Strang set for himself was to build a Northumbrian bagpipe, a complex instrument based on the French musette.

Gregory Walke, luthier

When he was a biology student, Gregory Walke visited Ireland with his brother Bernard. The trip proved to be a decisive experience as extended contact with traditional Irish music encouraged him to learn the violin and violin making. In 1979, Walke enrolled in the Welsh School of Violin Making and Repair in Great Britain, where he studied for three years. He furthered his knowledge during two training sessions in European workshops. In 1983, he was invited to spend a year studying and working in Michael Franke's workshop in Wiesbaden, Germany. Subsequently accepted in the Stuttgart workshop of master luthier and restorer Hieronymus Köstler, Walke spent two years learning the art of restoration and had the opportunity to work on major seventeenth- and eighteenth-century instruments. Upon returning to Canada in 1987, he opened a workshop with luthier Sibylle Ruppert and began collaborating with his brother Bernard, who is a bow maker. They have customers in Canada, the United States and Germany.

Karl Wilhelm,
organ builder

Karl Wilhelm learned to build organs in Germany and Switzerland, where he worked with the renowned organ makers Metzler and Sohne. He immigrated to Canada during the 1960s resurgence of organ building in Quebec, when the Casavant firm recruited European organ makers to revive tracker-action organs (which had not been built since 1904). In 1966, he established his own company, Karl Wilhelm Inc., in Mont-Saint-Hilaire. Staffed by a group of talented, specialized artisans, many trained by Wilhelm himself, his workshop is equipped to build all parts of the tracker-action organ and has produced over 120 organs, which have been sold throughout North America.

René Wilhelmy,
luthier

René Wilhelmy studied classical guitar at the Institut Marguerite Bourgeois and with guitarist Jean Vallières. During this training, he learned instrument making on his own, thus launching his career as a luthier. Two grants, one from the Canada Council and the other from the Office franco-québécois, enabled him to hone his skill, and his travels in Europe brought him into contact with major luthiers and guitarists. With his solid experience acquired over the years, Wilhelmy has become a prominent luthier.

While he works on historic guitar models, René Wilhelmy also experiments with building more modern instruments, such as folk guitars and electric guitars. To date, he has produced nearly one hundred instruments, including lutes, folk and electric guitars, and more than seventy-five classical guitars. These instruments, many of which are owned by award-winning musicians, are widely admired as much for their artistic beauty as for their fine tone.

General Bibliography

"Art du faiseur d'instruments de musique et lutherie," in *Encyclopédie méthodique, Arts et métiers mécaniques*. Geneva: Éditions Minkoff & Lattès, 1972 (reprint of 1785 ed.).

BACHMANN, Alberto. *An Encyclopedia of the Violin*. New York: DaCapo Press, 1966.

BOUCHARD, Antoine and André COUSINEAU. *Orgues au Québec*. Saint-Dié-des-Vosges: Organa Europae, 1991.

BOWLES, Edmund A. *La pratique musicale au Moyen-âge, Iconographie musicale*. S.l.: Éditions Minkoff & Lattès, 1983.

BRIL, Jacques. *À cordes et à cris, Origine et symbolisme des instruments de musique*. S.l.: Clancier-Guenaud, 1980.

BUCHNER, Alexandre. *Encyclopédie des instruments de musique*. Paris: Gründ, 1980.

COATES, Kevin. *Geometry, Proportion and the Art of Lutherie*. Oxford: Oxford University Press, 1985.

CONSTANT, Pierre. *Les facteurs d'instruments de musique. Les luthiers et la facture instrumentale, Précis historique*. Geneva: Éditions Minkoff, 1976 (reprint of 1893 ed.).

COTTE, Roger J.V. *Musique et symbolisme. Résonances cosmiques des instruments et des oeuvres*. S.l.: Éditions Dangles, 1988.

The Craftsman's Way, Canadian Expressions. Introduction by Hart Massey. Interviews and photographs by John Flanders. Toronto: University of Toronto Press, 1981.

D'AIGLE, Jeanne. *Histoire de Casavant Frères facteurs d'orgues, 1880–1980*. Saint-Hyacinthe, Quebec: Éditions D'Aigle, 1988.

Dictionnaire encyclopédique de la musique. Edited by Denis Arnold and Robert Laffont, 1988.

Early Keyboard Instruments. The New Grove Musical Instruments Series. S.l.: W.W. Norton & Company, 1989.

Encyclopedia of Music in Canada. Edited by Helmut Kallman, Gilles Potvin and Kenneth Winters. Toronto: University of Toronto Press, 1981.

EVANS, Tom and Mary Anne. *Guitars, Music, History, Construction and Players, from Renaissance to Rock*: New York: Facts on File Inc., 1977.

GIBBONS, Roy W. *CCFCS Musical Instruments Volume One: Aerophones*. Canadian Centre for Folk Cultures Studies Paper No. 43. Ottawa: National Museum of Man, 1982.

GIBBONS, Roy W. *CCFCS Musical Instruments Volume Two: Idiophones and Membranophones*. Canadian Centre for Folk Culture Studies Paper No. 44. Ottawa: National Museum of Man, 1983.

GIBBONS, Roy W. *CCFCS Musical Instruments Volume Three: Chordophones*. Canadian Centre for Folk Culture Studies Paper No. 45. Ottawa: National Museum of Man, 1984.

GRUNFELD, Frederic V. *Music*. New York: Newsweek Books, 1974.

HOLLINGER, Roland. *Les musiques à bourdons, vielles à roue et cornemuses*. Paris: La Flûte de Pan, 1982.

L'instrument de musique populaire, usages et symboles. Ministère de la Culture et de la Communication, Paris: Éditions de la Réunion des Musées nationaux, 1980.

Journal of American Musical Instrument Society, 1975–1991.

LASKIN, William. *The World of Musical Instrument Makers: A Guided Tour*. Photographs by Brian Pickell. Oakville: Mosaic Press, 1987.

LIBIN, Laurence. *American Musical Instruments in the Metropolitan Museum of Art*. New York: Metropolitan Museum of Art, 1985.

MAHILLON, Victor-Charles. *Catalogue descriptif et analytique du Musée instrumental du Conservatoire de musique de Bruxelles*. 5 vols. Brussels: Les amis de la musique, 1978.

MUNROE, David. *Instruments of the Middle Ages and Renaissance*. Oxford: Oxford University Press, 1976.

Musical Instruments in the Royal Ontario Museum. S.l.: Royal Ontario Museum, 1971.

Musical Instruments of the World: An Illustrated Encyclopedia by the Diagram Group. New York: Facts on File Inc., 1976.

The New Grove Dictionary of Musical Instruments. 3 vols. Edited by Stanley Sadie. London: Macmillan Press Limited, 1984.

SACHS, Curt. *The History of Musical Instruments*. New York: W.W. Norton & Company, 1940.

TAYLOR, Ronald Zachary. *Make and Play a Lute*. Hemel Hempstead, England: Argus Books Limited, 1983.

THORTON, Peter. *Musical Instruments as Works of Art*. S.l.: Victoria and Albert Museum, 1982.

TRANCHEFORT, François-René. *Les instruments de musique dans le monde*. 2 vols. Paris: Éditions du Seuil, 1980.

WINTERNITZ, Emanuel. *Musical Instruments and Their Symbolism in Western Art*. New Haven: Yale University Press, 1979.

YOUNG, Phillip T. *The Look of Music: Rare Musical Instruments, 1500–1900*. Vancouver: Vancouver Museums and Planetarium Association, 1980.

Selected Bibliography

Instrument Makers in Canada, 1971–1991

Compiled by Kevin James

This bibliography, compiled from surveys of periodicals and newspapers, lists articles written between 1971 and 1991 which contain substantive information on instrument makers active in Canada. Articles written before 1971 which were located in the course of the primary search have also been included. The sources consulted were vertical files and the index of Canadian music periodicals maintained by the Music Division, National Library of Canada; *Canadian Magazine Index* (1985–1991); *Canadian News Index* (1977–1991); *Canadian Periodical Index* (1977–1991); and *The Music Index* (1971–1991). The bibliography is arranged chronologically.

For well-documented subjects such as piano building, organ building and certain well-known makers (for example, electronic string-instrument maker Richard Armin, the organ builders Casavant Frères, violin maker George Heinl, the piano builders Heintzman & Co. and electronic-instrument inventor Hugh Le Caine), only the most substantial articles have been cited. The sparse documentation on brass- and woodwind-instrument makers indicates only that their work is relatively unchronicled and not that there is a lack of activity in Canada by such makers.

The compiler acknowledges the helpful assistance provided by the staff of the Music Division of the National Library of Canada.

Morin, Dollard. "Un expert canadien-français crée un piano électronique" [electric-piano inventor Oswald Michaud], *Le Petit Journal*, 20 May 1951.

"An extraordinary musician" [harpist and harp maker John Duncan], *CBC Times*, 24-30 June 1951.

Harbron, John D. "At Heintzman hustle replaces history" [piano builders Heintzman & Co.], *Executive*, vol. 3, no. 5 (May 1961).

"New sounds at Casavant" [organ builders Casavant Frères], *Time* [Canadian edition], vol. 81, no. 10 (8 March 1963).

Rochester, Rosemary. "Olé! For Canada's rebel guitar-maker" [Patt Lister], *Maclean's Reviews*, vol. 79, no. 8 (16 April 1966).

Bouchard, Antoine. "Casavant Frères – facteurs d'orgues depuis un siècle," *Forces*, no. 2 (Spring–Summer 1967).

Valpy, Michael. "After 100 years, a sour note as piano firm plays own coda" [Mason and Risch Ltd], *The Globe and Mail*, 11 March 1971.

"Violin maker Sid Engen brings home another prize," *Dauphin Herald* [Dauphin, Manitoba], 10 November 1971.

Bate, Michael. "New breed of composer writes space age music" [electronic-sackbut maker Peter Jermyn], *The Ottawa Citizen*, 26 February 1972.

Hickman, James. "David McLey: a new synthesizer composer," *The Canadian Composer*, no. 72, (September 1972).

Poitras, Harold. "Three-generation team makes old pipe organs hum again" [Caron organ rebuilders], *Montreal Star*, 7 October 1972.

"The instrument makers" [Jan H. Albarda, Christopher Allworth, John Bright, Casavant Frères, Ted Turner, The Instrument Shop], *Craftsman*, vol. 6, no. 1 (1973).

Hart, Matthew. "The Sackbut" [electronic-sackbut maker Peter Jermyn], *Weekend Magazine*, 16 June 1973.

Jamieson, George. "Heintzman: 123 years of tradition," *Music Canada Quarterly*, vol. 2, no. 2 (July–September 1973).

Bardsley, Alice. "No fiddling around: violin-making an art" [violin maker Jim McCleave], *The Atlantic Advocate*, vol. 64, no. 2 (October 1973).

Irving, Kit. "Sculpture to listen to . . . by Art Price" [musical-sculpture maker Art Price], *The Ottawa Journal*, 9 February 1974.

"Carving their own in B.C." [The Instrument Shop], *Time* [Canadian edition], 29 July 1974.

Thomson, Hugh. "Guitar maker Patt Lister keeps on trying for perfection," *The Globe and Mail*, 2 August 1974.

Laskin, Grit (William). "An interview with Jean Larrivée" [guitar maker], *Mariposa Folk Festival Newsletter*, March 1975.

"Just call him the master" [violin maker Eugene Breton], *The Hamilton Spectator*, 10 September 1975.

Gillmor, Alan. "Hugh Le Caine: a pioneer in electronic sound generation," *Canadian Composer*, no. 108 (February 1976).

"'Even a Stradivarius needs repairs'" [violin maker George Heinl], *The Toronto Star*, 27 February 1976.

McAlpine, Mary. "True to the harpsichord" [harpsichord maker Ted Turner], *Vancouver Sun*, 9 April 1976.

King, Paul. "Around Heintzman, the lady calls the tune" [Ann Heintzman of Heintzman & Co.], *The Toronto Star*, 2 October 1976.

McLean, Eric. "Introducing the Clavio" [keyboard-instrument maker Colin Kerr], *Montreal Star*, 23 October 1976.

"Gaston Ouellet est passé maître dans l'art de construire des clavecins," *La Musique Périodique*, vol. 1, no. 2 (December 1976).

Beker, Marilyn. "The computer maestro" [synthesizer composer and builder David McLey], *Weekend Magazine*, 18 December 1976.

"He's back at his hobby after 40 years" [violin maker David Laskey], *Winnipeg Tribune*, 15 January 1977.

Swimmings, Betty. "Organ builder" [Gabriel Kney], *The Ottawa Citizen*, 19 March 1977.

Emmerson, Frank. "The new harpsichord" [harpsichord maker Sigurd J. Sabathil], *Tempo*, vol. 1, no. 2 (May 1977).

Conlogue, Ray. "18th-century craft alive on Queen Street" [harpsichord maker John Hannaby], *The Globe and Mail*, 31 May 1977.

Dubuc, Madeleine. "Chez Casavant, la tradition d'abord" [organ builders Casavant Frères], *La Presse*, 23 May 1977.

Thistle, Lauretta. "Late Dr. Hugh Le Caine inventor of Canadian electronic instruments," *The Ottawa Citizen*, 9 July 1977.

"Home-made harpsichord" [maker John Herriott], *Evening Telegram* [St. John's], 15 October 1977.

Thibault, Jean. "Edgar Perrault, luthier," *La Voix* [Shawinigan-Grand'Mère], 16 November 1977.

Charbonneau, Daniel. "Des violons, il en fabrique et en joue" [violin maker Jules Saint-Michel (Gyula Szentmihaly)], *Perspectives*, vol. 19, no. 48 (26 November 1977).

"People" [harpsichord maker Harvey Fink], *Early Music Directory* [predecessor to *Continuo*], vol. 1, no. 5 (February 1978).

Duncan, Dorothy. "The Bell Organ Company," *Canadian Collector*, vol. 13, no. 2 (March-April 1978).

Bouchard, Antoine. "The organ in Canada: the first 300 years," *Musicanada*, no. 35 (April 1978).

Jew, Sandy. "Violin making: 'the master of the art'" [violin maker George Heinl], *Tempo*, June 1978.

Stevenson, Don. "Government loan refusal is sour note for piano firm" [Willis and Co.], *The Gazette*, 17 October 1978.

Colgrass, Ulla. "Violinmaker scoffs at 'Stradivarius sauce'" [Otto Erdész], *Music Magazine*, vol. 2, no. 2 (March–April 1979).

Canada Crafts special issue, vol. 4, no. 4 (April–May 1979):

> Bloom, Tony. "Divine winds" [wind-instrument makers Robert Fortier, Jack Goosman, Peter Noy and others].

> Bloom, Tony and Blair Ketcheson. "Handmade musical instruments today."

> Colgrass, Ulla. "Profile: Otto Erdész" [violin maker].

> "Drums of the Canadian Inuit."

> Hornjatkevyc, A.J. and T.R. Nichols. "The bandura" [bandura makers].

> Johnson, David. "Windharp" [Aeolian-harp maker].

> "Joseph Kun: focus on bowmaking."

> "Nexus" [new percussion instruments].

> Nurse, Ray. "Lutes" [lute maker].

> "Profile: E.R. Turner, harpsichord maker."

> "Profile: Wolfgang Kater" [harpsichord maker].

> "String section" [various makers].

Doig, John. "The music factory" [St. Thomas, Ontario, bagpipe maker Gordon Tuck], *The Canadian*, 9 June 1979.

Swimmings, Betty. "Piano firm remains a family affair" [Heintzman & Co.], *The Ottawa Citizen*, 6 October 1979.

"Letters: from Bob Marvin" [recorder maker], *Continuo*, vol. 3., no. 4 (January 1980).

Southworth, Jean. "Composer devises musical instruments" [Gayle Young], *The Ottawa Journal*, 9 April 1980.

Dewey, Martin. "Heintzman piano firm has played its part for 120 good and bad years," *The Globe and Mail*, 14 April 1980.

Carolan, Trevor. "Reviving a tradition: Vancouver's luthiers" [Michael Dunn, Michael Heiden, Bob Laughlin], *Open Door*, vol. 3, no. 9 (June–July 1980).

April, Pierre. "L'art de fabriquer des orgues . . . de père en fils" [Casavant Frères], *Le Droit*, 9 July 1980.

Miller, Mark. "Providing those pickers with something to pick" [Toronto exhibition *Measure for Measure*], *The Globe and Mail*, 8 November 1980.

Young, Gayle. "Hugh Le Caine: pioneer of electronic music," *Musicworks*, no. 14 (Winter 1981) [part 1] and no. 17 (Fall 1981) [part 2].

"People" [Halifax harp maker Reed F.Curry], *Continuo*, vol. 4, no. 4 (January 1981).

Harris, John. "Organ builder takes skills around world" [Gerhard Brunzema], *The Globe and Mail*, 19 January 1981.

Robert, Veronique. "Les orgues dans nos campagnes" [Casavant Frères], *L'actualité*, vol. 4, no. 12 (December 1981).

Lemery, Marthe. "Maurice Cellard démystifie l'art du luthier," *Le Droit*, 9 January 1982.

Le Page, Lorraine. "New instruments come from experimental urge" [composer Gayle Young], *St. Catharines Standard*, 28 January 1982.

Blashill, Lorraine. "At Fury, quality is everything" [guitar maker Glenn McDougall], *Saskatchewan Business*, vol. 3, no. 6 (January–February 1982).

Johnson, Brian D. "Melodic and rhythmic ghosts in the machine" [synthesizer composer and builder David McLey], *Maclean's*, vol. 95, no. 5 (1 February 1982).

Hawkins, Cameron. "David McLey" [synthesizer composer and builder], *Canadian Musician*, vol. 4, no. 2 (March–April 1982).

Musicanada special issue, "Instrument making in Canada," no. 48 (May 1982):

Barclay, Robert. "The conservation of musical instruments: a case for sentimental value."

Chalifoux, Sylvain. "Organ building in Canada: an export business."

Chatelin, Ray. "From electric guitars to harpsichords."

Young, Gayle. "Innovations in instrument design: the excitement of discovery."

Brunt, Stephen. "Building Thomson Hall organ a task for master craftsmen" [Gabriel Kney], *The Globe and Mail*, 22 May 1982.

Laskin, William (Grit). "Caught in a void: the instrument maker's dilemma," *Ontario Craft*, vol. 7, no. 2 (Summer 1982).

Knight, Irene G. "Sabathil & Son Ltd" [harpsichord makers], *Canadian Music Trade*, vol. 4, no. 3 (June-July 1982).

Leeper, Muriel. "New technology shapes genteel harpsichord" [harpsichord makers Sabathil & Son], *Music Magazine*, vol. 5, no. 4 (July–August 1982).

Cadesky, Eric V. "Cooking with glass" [Eric Cadesky, maker of glass percussion, wind and reed instruments], *Musicworks*, no. 21 (Fall 1982).

Young, Gayle. "The how and why of instrument building," *Musicworks*, no. 21 (Fall 1982).

Rimmer, Steve. "Linda Manzer: guitar builder," *Canadian Musician*, vol. 4, no. 5 (September–October 1982).

"People: Louis and Christiane Bégin" [bow makers], *Continuo*, vol. 6, no. 3, (December 1982).

Friesen, Michael D. "Canadian builds largest organ in U.S. church, 1870" [organ builder Louis Mitchell], *The Tracker*, vol. 27, no. 3 (1983).

Beck, Jenny. "Musician builds own pipe organ" [organ builder Herman Dost], *The Chronicle Journal* [Thunder Bay], 9 February 1983.

Geeza, John. "A new (18th century) organ for Redpath Hall" [organ builder Helmuth Wolff], *McGill News*, February 1983.

Siskind, Jacob. "Gold is pure music to this man's ears" [violin and bow maker Joseph Kun], *The Ottawa Citizen*, 4 February 1983.

Ellis, Patrick. "Sabian Cymbals Ltd," *Canadian Music Trade*, vol. 5, no. 2 (April–May 1983).

Kaptainis, Arthur. "Craftsmen of note" [violin makers Otto Erdész and Piet Molenaar], *The Globe and Mail*, 25 June 1983.

Dobbie, Mark and Luce Lamarre. "Luthier, faiseur d'instruments" [luthier Mario Lamarre and exhibition at Laval University], *Canadian Folk Music Bulletin*, vol. 17, no. 3 (July 1983).

Freedman, Adele. "Bravo highlights" [organ builder Gabriel Kney], *Bravo*, vol. 29, no. 6 (July-August 1983).

Rimmer, Steve. "Made in Canada," *Canadian Music Trade*, vol. 5, no. 6 (December 1983–January 1984) [part 1]; vol. 6, no. 2 (April–May 1984) [part 2]; vol. 6, no. 3 (June–July 1984) [part 3].

Guénette, Maryse. "Le démon de la collection – un amoureux de la musique" [violin maker Jules Saint-Michel (Gyula Szentmihaly)], *Châtelaine* [Quebec edition], vol. 25, no. 1 (January 1984).

Cooper, Frank. "About harpsichords: new faces" [Yves Beaupré], *The American Organist*, vol. 18, no. 2 (February 1984).

Wilson, Paul. "Ultra violins (and violas and cellos)" [Richard (Dick) Armin's electronic RAAD string instruments], *Shades* [Toronto], no. 33 (April–May 1984).

Mulaire, Bernard. "David and his harp: an historic Canadian organ case in Chicago" [organ builder Louis Mitchell], *Canadian Collector*, vol. 19, no. 3, May–June 1984.

Laskin, William (Grit). "Toronto instrument making," *Guitar Toronto* special issue, "Guitar 84 Festival Bulletin" (22–30 June 1984).

Strauss, Stephen. "Making music electronically" [Hugh Le Caine], *The Globe and Mail*, 25 June 1984.

Roback, Frances. "Research reports: advertising Canadian pianos and organs, 1850–1914," *Material History Bulletin* [Ottawa], no. 20 (Fall 1984).

Harris, John. "Two masters of a flourishing art" [organ builders Gerhard Brunzema and Gabriel Kney], *Music Magazine*, vol. 7, no. 4 (September–October 1984).

Laurier, Marie. "Hubert Bédard, facteur de clavecins anciens," *Le Devoir*, 8 January 1985.

Lavallée, Stéphane. "Yves Beaupré propose un son très particulier" [harpsichord maker], *La Tribune* [Sherbrooke], 19 January 1985.

McGrath, Paul. "Making a violin R2-D2 would enjoy" [Dick (Richard) Armin's electronic RAAD string instruments], *The Globe and Mail*, 23 March 1985.

Gould, Malcolm. "Heintzman pianos," *Canadian Music Trade*, vol. 7, no. 2 (April–May 1985).

McIntosh, Mary. "Jay Witcher's musical world" [harp maker], *Atlantic Insight*, vol. 7, no. 5 (May 1985).

Hall, Neal. "The instrument makers" [guitar maker Michael Dunn, period bow maker Kenneth Millard, African drum maker Themba Tana, harpsichord maker Ted Turner], *Vancouver Sun*, 4 May 1985.

Laskin, William. "Metro's music makers" [various instrument makers in metropolitan Toronto], *The Toronto Star*, 1 July 1985.

Brewer, Margot. "Status cymbals" [Sabian cymbal manufacturers], *Canadian Business*, vol. 58, no. 9 (September 1985).

Diemert, Christine. "The music maker" [violin maker William (Al) Gough], *Herald Sunday Magazine*, 10 November 1985.

"Discoveries and inventions" [electronic-sackbut inventor Hugh Le Caine], *Horizon Canada*, vol. 4, no. 42 (December 1985).

Seaman, Brian. "Reviving old music" [harpsichard and lute makers Tony Murphy and Will O'Hara], *Atlantic Insight*, vol. 7, no. 12 (December 1985).

"Why a luthier loves his job" [Winnipeg guitar maker Daryl Perry], *Vancouver Sun*, 20 January 1986.

"The finish is critical for guitar makers" [guitar maker George Gray], *Canadian Musician*, vol. 8, no. 1 (February 1986).

Kaetz, Deborah. "New guild luthiers" [harpsichord and lute makers Tony Murphy and Will O'Hara], *Consort* [Halifax], vol. 6, no. 4 (March 1986).

"Violin-maker pursues perfection" [Ted Obergan], *The Ottawa Citizen*, 12 April 1986.

Hunt, Steven. "One man's search for the perfect sound" [violin and bow maker Joseph Kun], *The Toronto Star*, 13 April 1986.

Burman, Terry. "Canadian guitar makers known world-wide" [various makers], *Canadian Musician*, vol. 8, no. 3 (June 1986).

Starr, Richard. "'The finest cymbals in the world': made in Meductic" [Sabian Ltd], *Atlantic Insight*, vol. 8, no. 10 (October 1986).

Edinborough, Arnold. "Electronic strings tuning up" [Richard (Dick) Armin's electronic RAAD string instruments], *The Financial Post*, 3 November 1986.

"Discoveries and inventions" [electric-organ inventor Morse Robb], *Horizon Canada*, vol. 8, no. 90 (January 1987).

Raphals, Philip. "Roll over, Stradivarius" [Dick Armin's electronic RAAD string instruments], *Science & Technology Dimensions*, première issue (January 1987).

Martens, Susan. "RAAD instruments rocking music world" [Dick (Richard) Armin's electronic string instruments], *Vancouver Sun*, 24 January 1987.

Gardner, Al. "Canadian luthier school opens" [Tugaske, Saskatchewan, guitar maker David Freeman], *Canadian Musician*, vol. 9, no. 1 (February 1987).

Bailey, Thomas and James Louder. "Christ Church. Oyster Bay, New York" [Helmuth Wolff and Associates], *The American Organist*, vol. 21, no. 5 (May 1987).

"Engineer designs updated dulcimer" [Cambridge, Ontario, dulcimer maker Bob Johnson], *Vancouver Sun*, 12 May 1987.

Muretich, James. "Craftsman's progeny music to customer's ears" [guitar maker Michael Heiden], *Calgary Herald*, 17 July 1987.

Lowry, William. "Joe Hugill keeps alive a family skill" [violin maker], *Hands*, vol. 7, no. 1 (Summer 1987).

Laurier, Marie. "Fernand Létourneau, facteur d'orgues québécois, se lance sur le marché international," *Le Devoir*, 12 September 1987.

Normand, Anne. "L'orgue de l'église de Saint-Césaire prêt à faire face à la musique" [Orgues Létourneau], *La Voix de l'Est* [Granby, Quebec], 26 September 1987.

Kirkwood, Heather. "Revolution in the big brass band" [acrylic-mouthpiece inventor Ellis Wean], *McGill News*, vol. 67, no. 4 (Fall 1987).

Young, Gayle. "Instrument innovations: the theory and design of a multi-intonational metallophone," *Percussive Notes* [Urbana, Illinois], vol. 26, no. 1 (Fall 1987).

Le Grand, Louis. "Denis Cormier, luthier québécois," *Le Devoir*, 24 October 1987.

Young, Gayle. "Twenty-four strings" [Gayle Young's amaranth] *Musicworks*, no. 37 (Winter 1987).

Staples, Michael. "A labour of love" [Millville, New Brunswick, harpsichord maker Eric Thulin], *New Brunswick*, vol 12., no. 3 (1988).

"Delta: Canada's only synthesizer maker," *Canadian Musician*, vol. 10, no. 1 (February 1988).

"Violin-maker has musical ear, runny nose" [Fredericton violin maker Clayton Boudreau], *The Ottawa Citizen*, 20 February 1988.

Brennan, Pat. "Baked in a kitchen oven this violin is a cool item" [engineer Leonard John and his graphite violin], *The Toronto Star*, 8 March 1988.

Besingrand, Franck. "L'orgue au Québec," *Sonances*, vol. 7., no. 3 (Spring 1988).

Koziara, Andrzej. "Musical classic: the violin is made today much as it was four centuries ago," *The Gazette* [violin maker Jules Saint-Michel (Gyula Szentmihaly)], 26 March 1988.

Buchignani, Walter. "Acrylic mouthpiece gives music new look" [tuba player and inventor Ellis Wean], *The Gazette*, 3 April 1988.

"Violins are sweet music to Gyula" [Montréal violin maker Gyula Szentmihaly (Jules Saint-Michel)], The Toronto Star, 5 April 1988; *Vancouver Sun*, 9 April 1988.

Conlon, Patrick. "In search of perfection" [violin maker Clayton Boudreau], *Your Money*, vol. 4, no. 6 (July–August 1988).

Keyser, Tom. "Master craftsman fashions beautiful music" [violin maker W.A. (Al) Gough], *Calgary Herald*, 26 November 1988.

Bartlett, Edouard. "Handmade for music: the instrument makers of Toronto," *Ontario Craft*, vol. 13, no. 4 (Winter 1988).

Trujillo, Ysabel. "Collins instrumental in keeping fine art of making violins alive" [Keith Collins], *This Week in Business*, vol. 1, no. 45 (3 December 1988).

Enchin, Harvey. "Beautiful music" [organ builders Casavant Frères], *Report on Business Magazine*, vol. 5, no. 4 (December 1988).

Scott, Michael. "Master craftsmanship makes instruments superb" [harpsichord makers Craig and Grant Tomlinson], *Vancouver Sun*, 10 December 1988.

Martel, Jacques. "Rencontre avec Denis Grenier" [percussion instrument maker], *l'ÉLAN*, vol. 1, no. 1 (Winter 1989).

"Rencontre avec Alain Beaudoin" [luthier and harp maker], *l'ÉLAN*, vol. 1, no. 1 (Winter 1989).

"Rencontre avec André Bolduc" [piano restorer], *l'ÉLAN*, vol. 1., no. 1 (Winter 1989).

"Rencontre avec André Gadoury" [violin maker], *l'ÉLAN*, vol. 1, no. 1 (Winter 1989).

"Rencontre avec Hubert Chanon" [violin maker], *l'ÉLAN*, vol. 1., no. 1 (Winter 1989).

"Rencontre avec Michel Fournelle" [electric-guitar and bass maker], *l'ÉLAN*, vol. 1, no. 1 (Winter 1989).

McDougall, Bruce. "Against all odds" [piano builder Sherlock-Manning], *Small Business*, vol. 8, no. 5 (May 1989).

"Un luthier expose sa collection" [violin maker Jules Saint-Michel (Gyula Szentmihaly)], *Le Devoir*, 9 May 1989.

"Un luthier montréalais qui recherche constamment la qualité" [Neil Hebert], *l'ÉLAN*, vol. 1, no. 3 (Summer 1989).

Burnette, J.A. "Canada journal: Sabian Cymbals, Meductic, N.B.," *Equinox*, no. 46 (July–August 1989).

Charette, Pierre. "Les luthiers du Québec . . . un peu d'histoire," [luthier Rosario Bayeur (1875–1944)], *l'ÉLAN*, vol 1., no. 4 (Fall 1989).

Cramer, Craig. "An interview with Gerhard Brunzema" [organ builder], *The American Organist*, vol. 23, no. 7 (July 1989).

Pedersen, Stephen. "Instrument-maker gains joy from craft" [Halifax folk-instrument maker Tom Dorward], *Halifax Chronicle-Herald* , 15 September 1989.

Simard, Francoise. "Richard Compartino: luthier-archetier," *l'ÉLAN*, vol. 1, no. 4 (Fall 1989).

Simard, Françoise and Kenneth Risdon. "Rencontre avec Pierre Laporte" [guitar maker], *l'ÉLAN*, vol. 1, no. 4 (Fall 1989).

Morgan, Jody. "Enlightening sounds" [harpsichord maker Tillmann Steckner], *Equinox*, no. 47 (September–October 1989).

Lyon, Nancy. "Vielle of fortune" [medieval wheel-fiddle maker Daniel Thonon], *Montreal Magazine*, no. 11 (December 1989).

Littler, William. "Canadian inventor opened musical windows" [electronic-instrument maker Hugh Le Caine], *The Toronto Star*, 31 March 1990.

Homer, Stephen. "Pipes of Glory" [organ builder Jean-Paul Létourneau], *Equinox*, no. 50, (March-April 1990); condensed version "Pipes of Glory" in *Reader's Digest* [Canadian edition], vol. 137, no. 820 (August 1990).

Kirk, Douglas. "An interview with Jean-Luc Boudreau," *Continuo*, vol. 14 [sic: vol. 15], no. 2 (April 1990).

Burford Mason, Roger. "Wood, metal and mechanical connections" [organ builder Gabriel Kney], *Musicworks*, no. 47 (Summer 1990).

Rogers, Corinne. "The search for authenticity in harpsichord making: an interview with Craig Tomlinson," *Musick*, vol. 12, no. 3 (December 1990).

"Otis Tomas: making instruments and tunes" [luthier and folk-instrument maker], *Cape Breton's Magazine*, no. 56 (1991).

Young, Gayle. "Playing the aural and the visual" [exhibition of sound sculptures], *Musicworks*, no. 49 (Winter 1991).

De Bièvre, Guy. "The improvisation moderator" [digital "trombone propeller" inventor Nicolas Collins], *Musicworks*, no. 49 (Winter 1991).

Roy, Vincent. "Denis Cormier — luthier et philosophie," *l'ÉLAN*, vol. 2, no. 6 (February 1991).

Roy, Vincent. "Stensland & Girard: une même passion, la lutherie," *Musicien québécois*, vol. 3, no. 1 (April 1991).

St. Amour, Colette. "Canadian-made guitars among world's finest" [William Laskin], *The Toronto Star*, 6 August 1991.

Enns, Ruth. "Material authenticity . . . of process" [luthier Ray Nurse], *Musick*, vol. 13, no. 2 (September 1991).

Enright, Robert. "Guitar man: the instrumental art of Murray Favro" [maker of functional art-design guitars], *Border Crossings*, vol. 10, no. 4 (November 1991).

Bédard, Romain. "Jean-Marc Forget scrute la mécanique du violon," *l'ÉLAN*, vol. 3, no. 5 (December 1991–January 1992).

Index of Instrument Makers

Index of Instruments